SERMONS
FOR SPECIAL DAYS

FREDERICK D. KERSHNER
M.A., LL.D.

SERMONS
FOR SPECIAL DAYS

BY

FREDERICK D. KERSHNER
M.A., LL.D.
PROFESSOR OF CHRISTIAN DOCTRINE IN DRAKE UNIVERSITY

NEW YORK
GEORGE H. DORAN COMPANY

TO
MY WIFE

PREFACE

The discourses which make up this volume have been delivered upon numerous occasions, and the oft repeated requests of sympathetic friends have led to their final appearance in the present form. The author has kept a record of the number of times several of them have been given, and in one case, at least, the figures run to over three hundred. He can only hope that the reception accorded by the readers of the book will be as kindly and sympathetic as the hearing given its subject matter when presented through the medium of the spoken word.

F. D. K.

Drake University
  Des Moines

CONTENTS

		PAGE
I	THE BATTLE OF LIFE	11
	[*A New Year's Sermon*]	
II	THE MAN WHO COUNTS	22
	[*Lincoln's Day Address*]	
III	IF WASHINGTON RETURNED . . .	34
	[*A Washington's Birthday Address*]	
IV	PASSION WEEK STUDIES	44
	1: Lessons from Gethsemane	
V	PASSION WEEK STUDIES	55
	2: Lessons from the Life of Judas	
VI	PASSION WEEK STUDIES	67
	3: The Greater Sin	
VII	THE ETERNAL QUESTION	79
	[*An Easter Sermon*]	
VIII	IDEAL WOMANHOOD	88
	[*Mother's Day Sermon*]	
IX	LIFE THROUGH DEATH	100
	[*A Sermon for Decoration Day*]	
X	THE SUPREME VIRTUE	111
	[*A Sermon for Flag Day*]	

ix

PAGE

XI THE UNREAD LESSONS OF LIFE . . 121
[*A Commencement Sermon*]

XII THE LIFE WORTH WHILE . . . 132
[*A Commencement Address*]

XIII THE EVOLUTION OF NATIONAL IDEALS 151
[*Independence Day Sermon*]

XIV THE MODERN WORSHIP OF MONEY . 162
[*Labor Day Sermon*]

XV THE DEATH OF THE GODS 173
[*An Address for Armistice Day*]

XVI GRATITUDE TRUE AND FALSE . . . 190
[*A Thanksgiving Day Sermon*]

XVII THE PROBLEM OF SUFFERING; AS RE-
LATED TO THE INCARNATION . . 200
[*A Christmas Sermon*]

XVIII THE END OF THE HARVEST . . . 212
[*A Sermon for the Last Day of
the Year*]

SERMONS
FOR SPECIAL DAYS

I

THE BATTLE OF LIFE

(*A New Year's Sermon*)

TEXT: *Rev.* 3:21. "To him that overcometh will I grant
to sit with me in my throne."

LIFE is one constant battle. From birth to death,
there is heard the sound of arms and the martial
tread of battalions. There is no station in society
nor any form of human activity in which this fundamental truth is not embodied. In the realm of
physical nature, as well as in the higher sphere of
mental ambition, and in the still higher circle of moral
heroism, the situation remains the same. Life in its
essence means striving, struggle and in the end either
victory or defeat.

I. *The Battle for Physical Existence.*

The battle begins with the struggle for existence in
the life of the little child. One disease after another

seeks to crush out the infant ere it has yet attained strength to survive. How anxiously the mother watches by the bedside of her babe while the breath comes and goes, and every moment to her trembling heart seems the last. Alas! her child is battling for life; simply beginning the first stage of what must be the history of its future career.

The young man, strong in the exuberance of perfect health, is every day conquering the germs of disease which are omnipresent in the world. The air is filled with a sort of floating tuberculosis and if we do not all die from consumption, it is chiefly because our physical constitutions are strong enough to fight off the insidious malady. Some years ago, the world of letters suffered the loss of one of the greatest educators of our modern age: Dr. William Rainey Harper, the first President of the University of Chicago. For many months, Dr. Harper had been battling for life with an incurable malady. Even up until the last moment, he directed the great work under his charge and fought with all the resources of science at his command in the hopeless struggle against disease. That he should lose the battle was of course inevitable, but his heroic defence excited the admiration and sympathy of the world.

It would be easy to multiply similar instances of gallant struggle against what may be styled the natural foes of the human race. History has unduly emphasised the heroism of another type of warfare, and we are accustomed, for the most part, to think of bravery only in connection with the roar of cannon and the shock of conflict upon the battlefield. Physicians and nurses, however, will bear testimony to the fact that the sublimest type of courage is often manifested in the more prosaic battle against disease. Occasionally this form of heroism receives its due measure of appreciation and fame. How breathlessly the American people watched the bulletins which told day after day of the long struggle for life made by James A. Garfield. In the remote corners of the United States, out on the prairies, and in little rural hamlets where only one or two newspapers were in circulation, the people gathered around the village postmaster and listened with attention while the details of the President's battle for life slowly, and often laboriously, were being read. Similar scenes were enacted, though not for so long a time, after the shooting of President McKinley. All over the country, the news concerning his battle for life was eagerly sought after and listened to with tear-stained eyes and lips which moved in silent prayer. Battling for life—yes, even physical life. For, whether conscious of it or not every one of us is at every moment engaged in a struggle for the very breath he or she draws; a struggle which must be kept up until death conquers at last.

II. *The Battle for Fame.*

Passing a step higher than the mere plane of physical existence, life exhibits a constant battle for fame and position. The annals of political history are simply the records of the life and death struggle of this man or the other for power and influence. Every nerve is strained, every latent power of body and mind brought into play in order that the victory may be won. Aaron Burr comes within one vote of supplanting Thomas Jefferson as President of the United States; but that defeat marks the climax of his career. James G. Blaine misses the goal of a lifetime's strenuous activity as the result of the chance remark of a comparatively obscure clergyman. But, however insignificant the cause, the fact and sting of defeat remain the same. Throughout the world, the tense struggle for fame and position is constantly going on with the pendulum swinging in one direction or the other. Political heroes are elevated and dethroned; and the idol of one hour becomes the next hour an object of neglect and scorn. Men have endured the most excruciating tortures simply to win a name. It is the opinion of the closest students of the ill-starred life of John Wilkes Booth, that but for this thirst for fame the most tragic crime of the nineteenth century would never have been committed.

Much of what passes for a higher motive in the national, in the social, nay even perchance in the religious realm, is at bottom only a selfish struggle for earthly distinction and renown. After all, the goal is a low one, for in a few hundreds, or at most a few thousands, of years, the fame of the greatest men approaches extinction. And what are a few hundred or a few thousand years in the timeless stretch of eternity? A traveller, wandering through the desert sands of Egypt, discovered an enormous statue lying broken on the ground. Upon the pedestal was inscribed, in hieroglyphics, these words: "Ozymandias, King of kings." We have practically no record of the career of this particular monarch, and few people to-day, even in the circles of the learned, would recognise his name. Nevertheless, he must have been a great man in his own time; a man who had worked ahead of all competitors in his own age. To-day, the vaunting epitaph upon his statue serves only as a text for the poet or the philosopher to illustrate the vanity of earthly ambition. There ought to be some higher and more lasting goal than fame; and there is. None the less in the realm of fame, the victory, such as it is, belongs, and belongs alone, to him who overcomes.

III. *The Battle for Heroism.*

Passing to a higher sphere, we reach what may be styled the battle for heroism. Here we approach something very different from the struggle for fame. The true hero is not concerned whether he wins a reputation or not; but, he is concerned that the principle for which he stands shall triumph. He knows that this triumph means, in every case, strenuous struggle and battle. A few years ago, on the twenty-third of May, I stood in the central square of Florence, Italy, to witness the celebration of the anniversary of the death of Savonarola, the great Italian reformer. There is an iron tablet located, it is said, upon the exact spot where a little over four hundred years ago Savonarola and his two companion monks were suspended from a gibbet and burned. On the day of the anniversary, the tablet was covered with banks upon banks of flowers. When, at the behest of the church which has since canonised him, Savonarola was led out of the little chapel where he had previously undergone the torture of the rack, across the platform, in front of the great Court Hall of Florence, and then up to the foot of the scaffold which like a huge cross stretched out its hideous arms into the Italian sunlight, I suppose his persecutors thought that they had put an end to his work. But they were mistaken. It is said that as Savonarola stood in the shadow of the scaffold and the black-robed priest pronounced the words of separation, saying according to the formula, "I separate thee from the church militant and triumphant," the hero of Florence turned about and replied in words that have justly become immortal, "From the church triumphant,—no! for the other I do not care." Savonarola was right— he belonged to the church triumphant. Out of the bitter agony of martyrdom his soul went up to receive the crown. He had heard the words of his Master, "To him that overcometh, will I grant to sit with me in my throne," and to him was granted the grace to overcome.

IV. *The Battle for Individual Character.*

The illustrations thus far given from the transitory battles for life, for fame, and for heroism on the part of the great and the good of the ages which have gone are but the fitting prototypes of our own individual struggles toward the goal. Every man and every woman is engaged day by day in a ceaseless battle to perpetuate the moral life. Temptations of every sort surround us; there are siren voices which whisper to us that we can relax our energy and still win the goal. The young man says to himself, "I will indulge in this or the other vice or dissipation and still preserve my character" not realising that the victory never belongs to the man who surrenders, but always to him who overcomes. By and by outside the breastworks of reputation, of honour, and of decent fame, he realises, when too late, the criminal folly of his career.

Much harm has been done by under-estimating the importance and the danger involved in the struggle for character. It has become customary nowadays for people to say "it's all the same any way"—there has come to be a sort of merging of the lines between vice and virtue in the minds of men and women of our modern age; a fatal blindness of soul which lulls them to forgetfulness until they awaken and find themselves in bondage to this or the other vice; enslaved to-day, and so far as we can see, enslaved forever. It is time for us to awaken from this false security and to realise that whatever we may say about the harmlessness of sin, or however we may apologise for pleasant and fair-seeming vices, there is no violation of God's law which does not carry with it its own penalty of bitterness and tears. "Stolen waters are sweet, And bread eaten in secret is pleasant. But he knoweth not that the dead are there; That her guests are in the depths of Sheol," and many a young man in the bitterness of

[17]

physical pain and moral condemnation has realised the wisdom of him who wrote these words. The path of virtue is not always a bed of roses but it is at any rate a highway undimmed by tears, and one which grows ever brighter and brighter until it leads into the majestic fulness of the perfect day.

Hence it comes that the supreme teachers and sages of the world have always emphasised what may be termed "the struggle side" of character-building. Always they have taught that life is a battle, that purity is not won without a struggle, that nobility carries its own scars upon its brow, above all that character itself is but the refined gold which flows out of the world's forges of temptation and affliction. Only the superficial and shallow interpreters of reality speak of the easy road to virtue. The Supreme Teacher, in his greatest recorded sermon, emphasises this lesson in the well known parallel between the pathway to life and the pathway to death. "Enter ye in," he says, "by the narrow gate: for wide is the gate, and broad is the way, that leadeth to destruction, and many are they that enter in thereby. For narrow is the gate, and straitened the way, that leadeth unto life, and few are they that find it."

V. *The Fate of the Slacker.*

In the battle for character, victory is always possible. In the external world, it is sometimes true that circumstances, over which we have no control, prevent us from achieving success. In the inner world of character values however, defeat can come in only one way and that is by abject surrender. Occasionally, we find men and women playing the part of the slacker, refusing to fight the battle, and in this way forfeiting their right to the crown. The great German poet Goethe has pictured the consequences of this attitude in Faust. The hero of the drama stumbles and falls many times but he is never completely lost because he never surrenders to the enemy. There is only one unpardonable sin in the universe and that is the sin of ceasing to want to be better than you are.

The young man who chooses to play the part of the slacker has chosen the least creditable part in the whole drama of existence—the part of the coward. Let him be assured, too, that he will always meet the coward's fate. Let him not delude himself with the idea that he will escape pain or discomfort by ceasing to strive for virtue. Everywhere in the universe, the most bitter expressions of suffering and agony rise from the hideous depths of the dens of sin. Life, after all, is much like that arrangement of certain of the ancient armies which placed behind the soldiers, platoons of their comrades armed with whips and swords to lash and, if need be, to kill the wretched stragglers who tried to steal away from the front. Leave the path of virtue because it seems hard and before you are aware the biting lash of sin will trace a scarlet mark across your cheek, and the iron of public and private condemnation will enter your soul, and the cruel rats of conscience and remorse will gnaw the peace out of your life forever.

VI. *The Lesson for the New Year.*

As we enter upon the new year, past experience teaches us that struggles and temptations await us. It is the part of wisdom to expect them and to be prepared to meet them. We should enter with optimism and cheerfulness, even with enthusiasm and with zest, upon the uncharted voyage which lies before us, knowing that if we are courageous and faithful victory must be ours in the end. Robert Browning in his somewhat difficult, and yet fascinatingly vivid, interpretation of the theme which is central in this sermon, entitled "Childe Roland to the Dark Tower Came" has taught the significance of courage and fidelity even under the most unfavourable surroundings. Perhaps few of us, during the coming year, will have to face discouragements as numerous or as trying as fell to the lot of the hero of the poem. In any event, we may be assured that like him we can conquer, if we never ground arms, and if we keep our place in the ranks, always striving, even though the battle be hard, for clean, upright, straightforward, Christian character.

After all, there is no escape from the battle no matter how hard we may try to avoid it. It is useless, in the spirit of Cain, to rebel against the manifest laws which govern our nature. Nor is there anything gained by repining or by reproaching destiny or the universe because the pathway has not been made easier for us. Such an attitude only makes what is hard still harder, and closes the road to ultimate happiness and success. Little by little, if we are patient and earnest

and true to the ideal which lights the way before us,
we shall pass through the valley of discouragement and
enter the glorious highlands of contentment and peace.
J. G. Holland, our own American poet, has pictured
the meaning and character of the process in simple but
unforgetable words:

> "Heaven is not gained at a single bound,
>   But we build the ladder by which we rise
> From the lowly earth to the vaulted skies
>   And we mount to its summit round by round.
>
> "I count this thing to be grandly true
>   That a noble deed is a step toward God
> Lifting our feet from the common sod
>   To a purer air and a higher view.
>
> "We rise by things that are 'neath our feet
>   By what we have mastered of good and gain
> By the pride deposed and the passion slain
>   And the vanquished ills which we hourly meet."

II

THE MAN WHO COUNTS

(*Lincoln's Day Address*)

THE story is told of a gilded youth who, after struggling for four years with the vicissitudes of college life, ultimately achieved a diploma. Proud in the possession of his new distinction he returned to the ancestral hearth, which happened to be located on a farm in the middle west, jauntily fitted out with an English plaid suit, a flashy tie, a large gold-headed cane, an eye-glass, and a Turkish cigarette. When his father saw him, he turned to a neighbour who was standing by and said: "In the language of Aaron in the wilderness: 'I poured in my gold and out there came this calf.'" From the results of personal observation, we are inclined to think that the farmer's criticism was not entirely without point. The type of individual which it portrays is not only formidable in numbers, but doubtless possesses distinct utility in certain important circles of our modern world. There are social functions, centres of popular amusement, and not a few more pretentious occasions which would be lost without him; and yet I think we will all agree that he scarcely represents the highest ideal of educational or spiritual ambition. Most of us will concede

that he is likely to be included among those to whom
the poet referred when he said:

> "For him no minstrel raptures swell
> But living shall forfeit fair renown
> And doubly dying shall go down
> To the vile dust from whence he sprung
> Unwept, unhonored and unsung."

In attempting to analyse the elements which constitute genuine success, we discover the one differentiating
feature to be the presence of some great purpose which
raises the man who possesses it above the petty level
of his own individuality, and makes him a sharer in
God's great work for the elevation of humanity. Some
one has said that the whole human family may be
roughly divided into four great classes. These classes
may be grouped after the following fashion: first, those
who do not count; second, those who count for little;
third, those who count in the wrong way; and fourth,
those who count for something worth while in the
right direction. We propose now to discuss these four
classes in the order named.

I. *The Class Which Does Not Count.*

The first class is perhaps the most numerous of all,
for the reason that it is the easiest one to enter. It
takes no special effort to amount to nothing and hence
the world is crowded with people who fulfil the conditions required for such a classification. These people do not belong to any one circle or station in society.
They are not even differentiated by the possession of
intelligence or natural ability. Some of the most

ss people with whom I am acquainted have
enough to accomplish almost anything. What
ifferentiate them from their really useful com-
is is the possession or lack of possession of some
consuming ideal for the world's betterment. They
have not learned the great lesson that in order to save
one's life, one must be willing to lose it; that what
really counts is not the nurture of a selfish personality,
but rather the complete abandonment of self in the
pursuit of something which is not individual but universal. Whenever a man can forget himself in the
pursuit of a supreme ideal, he has started on the pathway to real greatness. What counts is the ideal, what
does not count is the petty glorification of the individual. The man who throws himself with utter
abandon into the prosecution of some great purpose
is on the high road to become a man of destiny. He
has enlisted God and the universe on his side and his
own greatness is measured by the greatness of his
task.

There are certain classes of individuals who specifi-
cally do not count and cannot count. It may be well to
group a few of them together in order that the type
may be clearly discerned. All of them represent the
embodiment of some selfish feature which does not
rise beyond the narrow limits of their own personali-
ties. There is, for example, the incarnation of selfish
pride, the man whose one ambition appears to be to
display himself to what he conceives to be the best
possible advantage. If this desire takes the form of
personal appearance, we style the individual in ques-

tion a "dude." To such a being, the cut of his clothes or the colour of his necktie is of more significance than the triumph of right or the victory of truth over falsehood in the world. His gods are the tailor and the barber, and the temple in which he worships is the drawing-room. He repents in sackcloth and ashes if his shoes are not shined, but he is callous as a side of sole leather to spots on his soul which the angel Gabriel could not wipe off if he worked at the task with unintermittent vigour from now until the day of judgment. Of such an individual, the most charitable comment which one can make is the remark of Portia to Nerissa, "God made him therefore let him pass as a man."

Another class which does not count is the class which represents the incarnation of selfish ease. The man who belongs in this group is the man whose conception of heaven is a large armchair with a plush bottom and a rest for his feet. The only hell which he can conceive is a place where for some reason or other he will be obliged to work. If he could be assured that there will be no coal to shovel in hades, he would willingly engage a reservation in some secluded spot in the lower world where he could sit down throughout eternity. His attitude reminds one of the chorus of the old negro plantation hymn which used to run "I wish I was in heaven a sittin' down, a sittin' down." He embodies perhaps the most useless of all forms of selfishness, the selfishness of indolence.

Still another group which does not count is the group which represents the incarnation of selfish pleasure.

The man who belongs to this group is the man whose one ambition in life is "to have a good time." What he means by a good time is the limitless gratification of his own material pleasures. His one rule of conduct is, "eat, drink and be merry, for to-morrow we die." So far as the good of humanity is concerned, the sooner to-morrow comes the better it is for the world. It is the characteristic of most animals that they serve the uses of civilisation more by their death than by their life, and this type of animal is no exception to the rule. He differs from the other animals, however, in this respect that he is of no particular use either dead or alive.

We trust that what has been said will not be regarded as purely caricature. There is no greater tragedy conceivable than a wasted and misused life. That a being created in the image of God should deliberately, or otherwise, forfeit his heritage, is the saddest fact in human history. Whenever such a tragedy occurs, in almost every case it is due primarily to one cause. This cause is the pursuit of individual selfishness. God is the one completely unselfish Being in the universe and man has the choice of climbing toward him by following the path of an unselfish ideal, or of sinking to the level of the brute by pursuing the brute's own pathway of incarnate selfishness. During the recent war, the vocabulary of the average individual was enriched by a number of new words. One of the most universally used of these expressions was the ignominious term "slacker." The word came into general use before conscription was adopted in England and was employed to characterise the men who refused to volunteer in order to bear their share of the great national burden. These men were justly despised for the reason that the cause of freedom or of justice made no appeal to them. Their one concern was to save their own miserable lives, no matter how many of their neighbours or townsmen were dying in the trenches. The devil characterised them aptly when he said, "Skin for skin, all that a man hath will he give for his life." The man who prizes his own life or ease more than honour, duty or justice is a slacker. Moreover, the slacker represents the type of man who does not count and never has counted in the history of the world.

II. *The Class Which Counts for Little.*

When we turn to the second class of people who make up humanity, the class which counts for little, we find that what differentiates them from the first class is the partial possession of an ideal which goes beyond their own selfish personality. The criticism which the world passes upon them is that the possession of this ideal is only partial. Many of them start out well but for some reason or other they speedily fall by the wayside. Here, for example, is a man who begins his career with high ideals of service, but after a time he becomes engrossed in the affairs of the world to such an extent that he loses his early standards. There are a number of reasons which may be responsible for this situation. One of the most common causes is the simple stress of circumstances. A man can so surround himself with selfish conditions that he can scarcely escape the poison of their influence. It requires constant effort to keep high ideals alive even on the part of the best of us, and if we deliberately neglect the means of fostering them we cannot hope to preserve our higher standards. Herein may be found one of the great arguments for church affiliation and attendance. By associating ourselves with those who are striving to keep alive the nobler principles of conduct, we make it easier to follow in the same pathway. On the other hand, by cutting ourselves off from the benefit of these associations, we are apt to sink speedily to the lower level. It should never be forgotten that men very largely create their own environment. If we deliberately choose to foster conditions which destroy our higher aspirations, we have no right to complain when these aspirations disappear.

Another cause of the loss of the higher motives is intellectual scepticism. I knew a young man who became absolutely valueless, who lost all of his zeal for service and his enthusiasm for better things because he plunged headlong into a course of sceptical reading and had not stability enough to keep his balance. He had the making of a great man in him but he lost his faith in goodness and in God, and he dropped back into a life of nothingness. A man's reading will mould his life no less surely than will his actual associates. The old idea was that it did not make much difference what a boy or girl read, just as the old idea was that flies and mosquitoes were innocent creatures bearing a

[28]

special commission from the Deity to bite you and thus chasten your disposition. We have learned now, however, that the fly and the mosquito got their passports crossed, so to speak, and instead of coming from the Deity as special harbingers of his grace, their starting-point was somewhere else; and yet it is just as reasonable to expose a child recklessly to typhoid bearing flies or to yellow fever mosquitoes as it is to give him thoughtlessly a certain type of literature to read. Mosquitoes may poison the body but bad books poison the soul. If you want to lose your spiritual and moral power, and cut the tendons of the higher life and ultimately come to amount to nothing in the world, just select the wrong kind of reading material and keep reading it.

III. *The Class Which Counts in the Wrong Way.*

We pass now to the third group, the class which counts, but which counts in the wrong way. These people have learned the lesson that success means the pursuit of a great ideal, but they have been unfortunate in their choice of ideals. They have hitched their wagon to a star, as Emerson expressed it, but the star turns out to be one of the wandering kind mentioned by the Apostle as delusions reserved for "the blackness of darkness forever." Saul of Tarsus started out as one of these people but fortunately reversed his life before it was too late and thus escaped the rapids. Men of this kind are always marked out for greatness even though it be greatness in the wrong way. The collapse of modern civilisation in the world war, for example, was largely due to the mistaken ideals of three men. The first of the three was named François Arouet, later styled Voltaire. Voltaire was a man of extraordinary brilliancy of intellect who honestly reacted against the hideous superstition which in his day masqueraded under the name of Christianity. He made his life the embodiment of a protest, a protest as mistaken as the thing against which he protested. He lived to see himself the idol of the French people and at the age of eighty, to receive the plaudits of almost the united populace of Paris. There can be no question that Voltaire's life counted and that it still counts to-day. But it counted in the wrong direction. It made France largely a nation of atheists and crippled her irreparably in the struggle for existence among the peoples. Its influence went beyond France and helped to build up that trust in materialism which has been the chief source of moral decadence for over a century.

The second man whose influence has pre-eminently moulded thought in Europe in the wrong way was Napoleon Bonaparte. Like Voltaire, Napoleon reacted against a false system. He became the political idol-breaker as Voltaire became the religious iconoclast. Like Voltaire, he threw himself into the pursuit of the ideal which attracted him, and for this reason climbed to the heights of renown. But Napoleon, too, followed a false ideal in the end. He built up for Europe the spell of a militaristic empire which has not yet passed away. Instead of following the example of

[30]

Washington or of Cromwell, he preferred to revive the ideals of Cæsar, and Europe is paying the price to-day. Napoleon's life counted but it counted in the wrong direction. It will be a long time before the world is entirely free from the baleful influence of his programme of blood and iron and ambition.

The third man whose influence is cursing the world to-day was the half-crazed son of a Protestant minister of Germany who, disappointed in an early friendship, reacted against all idealism and proclaimed his adherence to the gospel that might makes right and that power is the only goal worth while in the world. With all his faults, Friedrich Nietzsche was a prophet, though a prophet of the wrong kind. His life counted and it still counts. His doctrines, perhaps more than the teachings of any other one man, helped to furnish the intellectual basis of modern German materialism. To Voltaire who helped to destroy religion, to Napoleon who aimed to substitute the glitter of a military aristocracy for genuine democracy, and to Nietzsche who sapped the foundations of moral idealism and of altruism and substituted for them a gospel of ruthless physical force, the world to-day owes chiefly the disease of hatred and of strife which threatens the very existence of civilisation. The political, the moral and the religious elements constitute the framework of the social order. Napoleon attacked the political, Nietzsche the moral, and Voltaire the religious; and the three together have come very near wiping out the whole structure of human society.

IV. *The Class Which Counts in the Right Way.*

It is a relief to turn to the final group of people who make up the universe—the class which counts and which counts in the right direction. These are the people who have chosen a really noble ideal and have devoted their lives to its service. It is to such souls that the poet referred when he said:

"There are loyal hearts, there are spirits brave,
There are souls that are pure and true;
　Then give to the world the best you have,
And the best will come back to you.
　Give love, and love to your heart will flow,
A strength in your utmost need;
　Have faith, and a score of hearts will show
Their faith in your word and deed."

Men of this kind count and they count for what is highest and noblest and best in the world. Paul of Tarsus was essentially one of this group. His whole life was simply the incarnation of a sublime ideal, an ideal which consumed all thoughts of self and of selfish ambition. Among those who belong in the same category were Francis of Assisi, Savonarola, Martin Luther, Joan of Arc, Oliver Cromwell, David Livingstone, Frances Willard, and scores of others. It was characteristic of all of these great figures that they reckoned not their own lives as being of special significance in comparison with the prosecution of the ideals for which they stood. Hence, their lives counted and still count in the onward march of world history.

There is no figure in the annals of secular life who so thoroughly embodies the principle to which we have been referring as does Abraham Lincoln. John Drink-water, the English dramatist, has recently portrayed the life of this remarkable character in the most compelling fashion. He shows us a man whose one thought and purpose and ambition was to serve the highest need of his people and his generation. No other figure in American history, not even the immortal Washington, was so completely unselfish, so utterly oblivious to personal ambition and personal pleasure, as was the hero of Springfield. No other man in modern history possessed the capacity for over-looking personal slights and discourtesies to the same degree as did Abraham Lincoln. His relations with Stanton alone furnish a commentary upon magnanimity which can scarcely be duplicated in the world's history. The careful student of his state papers, especially the second inaugural address and his speech at Gettysburg, will note how thoroughly he subordinates all personal considerations to the over-mastering ideal which had become the consuming passion of his life. No other man in modern life has counted for more than Abraham Lincoln, and the chief reason for his pre-eminence is to be found in the fact above stated. Of him, it may be truthfully said that Mark Antony's famous panegyric upon Brutus finds complete realisation in actual experience:

> "His life was gentle, and the elements
> So mixed in him that nature might stand up
> And say to all the world, this was a man."

III

IF WASHINGTON RETURNED

(*A Washington's Birthday Address*)

IT is said that an Irish usher was approached by a young lady at a crowded concert in New York City with the request for a seat. "Indeed, miss," replied Pat, "I should be glad to give you a seat but the empty ones are all full." When one is looking for something new to say about George Washington, he is apt to find the empty seats all full. Shades of Fourth of July and twenty-second of February orations in countless numbers arise before him and with their hollow echoes, mostly hollow, disturb his peace of mind. Everything seems to have been said on the subject that can be said and perhaps a little more. And yet, the life of Washington, like that of every other truly great man, possesses a value that is in its own way inexhaustible. There is always room for one more commentary on Homer, one more essay on Shakespeare, one more life of Napoleon. A half million or more sermons a week for over a thousand years have not sufficed to exhaust the Bible as a storehouse of inspiration. All genius is in truth of such a miraculous and divine quality that, like the cruse of the Shunammite woman, it can never be drained dry.

The book which you have read through possesses a new value when you read it again. The letters seem aglow with a new message. The flaming pens of the unseen cherubim who are the guardian angels of inspiration have re-written the pages while you were asleep. A book that will not stand a third reading is not worthy of the first. It is a sin against opportunity to read most of the transient literature to-day, and it is likewise a criminal waste of time. What is true of books is also true of men, for books are but the crystallised life, the congealed blood, as it were, of their authors.

I. *The Return of Washington.*

A good many years ago, Mr. William T. Stead, at that time the editor of the *Pall Mall Gazette* of London, paid a visit to the pork-packing metropolis of the universe and speedily poured forth his impressions in a volume entitled "If Christ Came to Chicago." Mr. Stead was a good newspaper man and he started a distinct fad in titles. In a short time, we had books entitled "If Christ Came to Congress" and a host of other imitations of the kind. Some of these works, while pretending to be defenders of virtue, were in reality little more than guide books to vice. However legitimate the idea may have been when used with reference to the founder of Christianity, it is certainly worth consideration when applied to the first great American. Some years ago in the City of Philadelphia, there was celebrated the bi-centennial of the birth of Benjamin Franklin, the man who occupies a position perhaps second only to Washington among our early heroes. As I recall it, one of the principal features of the celebration was the conferring by the University of Pennsylvania, of the degree of Doctor of Laws upon His Majesty, King Edward of England. They made him Doctor Edward the Seventh. When I read the newspaper account, I wondered what Ben Franklin would have thought if he could have come back to Philadelphia while the celebration was going on. It is true that he tried to doctor His Majesty, George the Third, but it was in a different way. He was over at the Court of France most of the time fixing up prescriptions of powder and shot for the benefit of His Royal Highness.

Some time ago I visited the scene of the battle of Lexington, the first contest in the war of 1776. They told me, reviving memories of my old school history, of how the red coats marched out of Boston in the dead of night in order to destroy the stores of ammunition at Concord. As the boatload of soldiers embarked at the foot of Boston Common, the lantern swung out of the old North Church and sent its warning to the patriots on shore. As I stood there, I saw in imagination the sunrise gilding the Massachusetts hills, while on all sides were heard the booming of guns and the ringing of bells to arouse the people. And then, in the quiet village square at Lexington, I saw the little band of seventy men from the fields assembled on the green in front of the church, without breastworks or any special means of defence, to dispute the passage of four hundred and fifty regulars of the army of King George. On come the red coats, marching at double quick time, Major Pitcairn on his white horse riding before. The seventy men do not falter. "Disperse, ye rebels," cries Pitcairn waving aloft his sword. There is the silence of death for a moment. It is one of those occasions when Time stands still and Destiny puts her finger upon her lips. The old church is peaceful as the grave. The swallows twitter on the roof. The moment passes, and with its passing a new era in the history of humanity begins. "Fire," roars Pitcairn and the volley heard round the world rings out. A third of the seventy fall dead and wounded to the ground; the remainder disperse. The soldiers of King George fire another volley and give three cheers for their victory, while the dying Americans writhe upon the grass. Those cheers are heard likewise around the world. Over in Connecticut, they waken Israel Putnam from his lethargy; in Vermont, they sound like a clarion call to Ethan Allen; in Virginia, they tingle through the blood of Washington.

These things took place less than a century and a half ago. If Washington could come back to America to-day, what would he say of the nation which had such an humble beginning on the village green of Lexington. I have no doubt but that he would be very much gratified at the progress we have made. There were no railroads when he was alive, no telegraph or telephone lines, to say nothing of the wireless; no steamships, no aeroplanes, in fact none of the achievements of modern invention and industry. A dozen San Francisco earthquakes might have come and gone and we would have been none the wiser. Great cities have sprung into existence where only the trackless forests stretched before. Strange reminiscences would throng his mind as he passed along. Where once amid the silence of the night and by the flickering light of a single torch, he read the funeral service over the dead body of Braddock, there is now a city of nearly a million inhabitants. Instead of the hoot of the owl, there is heard the shriek of the locomotive; the forests have become harvest fields; the huts of the red men, palaces of brick and marble. "A great nation," I can imagine he would say, "well worth the blood shed upon Bunker Hill and the bitter privations of Valley Forge."

II. *The Criticism of Washington.*

More significant to us perhaps than the commendation of Washington, would be his criticism. There are certain things in our American life to which, we can hardly doubt, he would take exception. One of them would be our fawning upon and servile imitation of the degenerate aristocracy of other nations. Let a decayed duke or a no account count come into the United States and he can scarcely get out of the country without taking several millions of American money, with the millionaire's daughter thrown in as a trivial accompaniment. If George Washington saw perhaps our most representative metropolitan hotel and by chance asked where the owner was, he would be told that he was over in Europe begging to be allowed the privilege of paying the gambling debts of certain aristocrats whose ancestors the father of our country helped to kick across the Atlantic in 1776 and 1777. What do you suppose Washington would have to say about such a situation? I do not know what he would say but I feel reasonably sure of what he would think. He would think of that scene which took place within gunshot of the same hotel a little over a hundred years before it was built. He would think of that terrible day, the most bitter in his life, when, telescope in hand, he watched from the American entrenchments the slaughter of Sullivan's troops upon Long Island. Again he would see Smallwood's Maryland brigade, surrounded by ten times their number, charge in vain upon their foes. He would hear the distant shouts of triumph ringing over the hills of Flatbush and once more in imagination he would drop his telescope and cover his face with his hands and cry out, "My God, my God, what brave men must I lose to-day!" He would think too of the bitter sadness which followed the night of the battle; of the long anxious moments of suspense and danger while the disheartened troops were ferried across the East River; of the delegations of women and children who came to him begging him to save their city and homes. I am not trying to arouse any feeling against Great Britain as a nation or against the British people as a people in uttering these words. What I am trying to do is to protest with all the earnestness of my soul against the miserable snobbishness which cringes in the dust before foreign titles and which apes, at whatever cost, foreign customs. I have lived in England and I know that no self-respecting Englishman would think of being guilty of such a treason against his native land; no self-respecting Italian would do it; not even a self-respecting China-man; and, wherever born, the man who lives in the United States and does it, is not and never was an American.

Another thing which I think would grieve the spirit of Washington if he were to come back to his native land is the mad materialism of our social and political life. We are coming perilously near to the condition pictured by the old moralist when he said of a certain class that they "lived for the lust of the moment and died in the doing of it." One class in our social order apes the class just above it, and that one apes the one above it, until the highest class in this infamous competition apes some titled numbskull who sets the fashion across the Atlantic. Instead of making our social customs—our dress or our habits of life our servants as they should be, we have made ourselves their slaves. Men toil night and day to keep up a certain style of living because somebody else does the same thing, and somebody else does the same thing because somebody else does it. We wear out our lives in this useless competition. It is no discredit not to have much money. The wisest, bravest and best of the men of earth have been poor—from Homer, who was a beggar, to Jesus Christ who owned only a single garment when he died. But it is a disgrace which ought to sear your very brain to try to imitate some one who has more money than you have. You are his equal, perhaps his superior, as long as you assert your independence, but the minute you begin to imitate him, he treats you as what you are; that is, his inferior. This is particularly true of dress. If you dress as becomes your means, he respects you; in fact, you compel his respect. But if you try to ape him, he mistakes you, as he has a right, for his footman. One of the most admirable things about the character of Robert Burns was his independence. He had some very serious faults but there was nothing servile about him. When the high society of Edinburgh took him up as a sort of curiosity and made a great todo over him, he never sacrificed his independence by toadying before them. He was altogether different from the people of the present day whose chief ambition in life appears to be to be kicked by somebody who has been kicked by somebody who has wandered over the threadbare kingdoms of Europe imploring the nobility to kick him.

There are other things which would cause Washington regret but the limits of the present address do not permit their mention. Among them might be named the enslavement of the people by certain forms of corporate wealth, the curtailment and at times the destruction of the freedom of the press and of public assembly, the enormous centralisation of governmental functions, the widespread prevalence of graft and other evils which have followed in the wake of our national and civic development.

III. *Washington and England.*

There is one phase of present-day life in America which demands especial attention in any study of the life of Washington. This is the changed attitude of American sentiment toward the English government and the English people. Reference has been made to the criticism which we must believe the father of his country would visit upon those Americans who are willing to sacrifice their independence in exchange for a titled mess of pottage. While this is true, we cannot help feeling also that he would rejoice in the increasing solidarity of the Anglo-Saxon race. Washington was thoroughly English by birth and it was only the stubborn folly of a pedantic Hanoverian despot which drove him to take up arms against his own blood kindred. The fact of the case is that George the Third was a great deal more German than he was English. In order to enforce his tyrannical dictates upon his subjects in America, the half-insane old Teuton was fain to employ a considerable body of Hessian mercenaries. These Hessians later came to grief in much the same fashion as was true of their descendants in the recent world war. The real spirit of England, that is of the Anglo-Saxon peoples, was always sympathetic with Washington. It was only extraneous conditions which produced the line of cleavage which divided England from America in the days of the Revolution. We should all of us rejoice, and we feel sure that George Washington would himself rejoice most of all, if he could return, in the changed attitude which has come over Anglo-American relations. John Drinkwater, the English dramatist, who has so admirably interpreted the ideals of Abraham Lincoln, has likewise brought a message of affectionate greeting to the descendants of Washington. Perhaps no American author has appraised the worth of the hero of Mt. Vernon more sympathetically and more completely than Englishmen like Drinkwater and Bryce. For this recognition, the Father of his Country would doubtless be grateful if he could return. In the consciousness of unity between the great English-speaking nations, he, like other prophets of the dawn, would recognise the approach of "that far-off divine event toward which the whole of creation moves."

IV

1: *Lessons from Gethsemane*

TEXT: *Mark* 14:32. "And they came to a place which
was named Gethsemane."

THE story of the Scriptures is largely a story of
gardens. It begins in Genesis with the Garden
of Eden with its vision of innocence enshrined amid a
bower of roses and daffodils, and it closes in Revelation with a picture of the garden of God that shall
become the Paradise of the redeemed. Humanity, with
its misery and sin, is bounded on each side by flowers.
Eden and Paradise are both pictured as gardens, and
between the regret for the garden that has faded and
the longing for the garden that is to be revealed lies
the checkered pathway of the sons of men.

Midway between the two gardens of the past and
of the future, we come to another which we all shrink
from entering. As we read the title over the gate,
fear and anguish overwhelm us for it is the dreaded
garden of Gethsemane. Escape it, we cannot for our
pathway lies straight on. The road has closed behind
us. On both sides, impassable precipices rear themselves. There is but one path for us and that path is
through the garden. Ella Wheeler Wilcox has pic-

tured in unforgetable fashion the inevitableness of Gethsemane.

> "Down shadowy lanes, across strange streams
> Bridged over by our broken dreams;
> Behind the misty caps of years,
> Beyond the great salt fount of tears,
> The garden lies. Strive as you may,
> You cannot miss it in your way.
> All paths that have been, or shall be,
> Pass somewhere through Gethsemane.
>
> "All those who journey, soon or late,
> Must pass within the garden's gate;
> Must kneel alone in darkness there,
> And battle with some fierce despair.
> God pity those who cannot say,
> 'Not mine but thine,' who only pray,
> 'Let this cup pass,' and cannot see
> The purpose in Gethsemane."

Gethsemane represents the never-ending struggle between the spirit and the flesh, between the higher and the lower natures, between the weakness of the human and the aspiration toward the divine which is characteristic of every step upward in character.

I. *Gethsemane and Human Friendships.*

It is noticeable when we first come to the garden that, like the Christ, we have all of our friends with us; but as we enter beneath the low-roofed archway, we voluntarily elect to leave most of them behind. It is said that sorrow loves company, but it is certainly true that it does not love too much company. The bitter agony which wrings our hearts shrinks from the publicity of even the gaze of friendship. Perhaps most of our friends would not care to go with us any way, for as a rule human ties break when tested by misfortune. But even if they desired to enter, we would not want them. And yet while this is true of the great bulk of those whom we style our friends, it is likewise true that there will always be one or two or three of those we love best that we will take with us into the garden. They are our old and trusted acquaintances, those whose devotion we have proved, and of whose fidelity we are assured. They are, like Peter and the two sons of Zebedee, the men and women we have known longest and loved best; and in this hour of bitterness, "When our souls are exceeding sorrowful even unto death," we cling to them as we have never clung to them before.

Moreover, our chosen friends are satisfied to watch and to do what they can for us even though they cannot understand nor appreciate the grief which weighs us to the ground. It is a fact as universal as human nature itself, that no matter how kind-hearted or sympathetic we may be, we never thoroughly understand the grief of another person nor does any other person ever understand our grief. The deepest springs of sorrow find their sources in the fountain depths of the heart and are never disclosed to the eye of another. Men have sometimes said that the longing for sympathy is sheer weakness, but these men do not themselves escape from it and, like the Nazarene, they will always be found eager to lean upon their closest friends when the final moment of trial comes. Friends—how comforting the word sounds to us!

In our days of gaiety and pleasure, we did not need them. On the triumphal march from Bethany with the flowers blooming by the roadside and the bright sun shining overhead, we could have gotten along without them; but now in this cold drear garden, with its twisted and gnarled olive trees, and the sharp flints which pierce our feet, to say nothing of the misery which weighs upon our hearts, we want friends as we have never wanted them before. Gethsemane is bad enough with a companion or two to help to ward off the spectres that assail us, but Gethsemane alone is more than we can bear. So we say, but alas, it must be Gethsemane alone. We look around for our companions only to find that they are all asleep, and then the sense of our abandonment comes upon us with double severity. They are tired, of course, but are we not tired too? And yet can we sleep? If they felt or could feel the thousandth part of the bitterness which is ours, sleep would be as impossible for them as for us. But they do not feel it—the conclusion is forced upon us with inevitable certainty—and so we realise that our Gethsemane must be borne alone.

It is said that during the darkest hours of the War between the States, a stranger happened accidentally to enter the private room of Abraham Lincoln. He found the President upon his knees with the tears streaming from his eyes. Before the world, Lincoln was a man of imperturbable coolness, usually masking his thought behind the protecting cover of some criticism or jest. But Lincoln, we may be assured, had his

Gethsemanes, and we may be assured too that he passed through them alone.

II. *The Universality of Gethsemane.*

Of all the lessons in the life of Christ, there is none more universal than is the lesson of Gethsemane. On the mountain top of Transfiguration, he is raised above us and we can scarcely understand the reality of his glory. As a worker of miracles, he is divine rather than human. In his temptation, even, where he seems to descend nearest to our human level, he is still so far above us that we despair of understanding him; but here in the garden, where the spirit struggles with the flesh, where he longs for human sympathy and manifests so much of our own human nature, here, it seems to me, he becomes intensely real.

It will be observed that Jesus experiences the double shock of finding the disciples twice asleep in the garden. The gospel narratives differ in their interpretation of the circumstance. Luke says that they had fallen asleep because of sorrow; Mark because their eyes were heavy, "neither wist they what to answer him"; Matthew reiterates the statement of Mark. There is no real disagreement in the narratives since they portray only different sides of the same thing. Their eyes were heavy because they were tired out with the watching of the previous nights of the Passover. They were sorrowful and had wept at the sadness of their Master—a sadness which they could not understand and which they could not relieve. Most of all,

I think their feeling is portrayed in the quotation, "they wist not what to answer Him," one of the most pathetic lines contained in the Scriptures. There is a drama sometimes enacted in real life which conveys an idea of what that line means. A mother, whose heart is wrung with anguish because of the death of her husband, is weeping beside her child. The latter, who is old enough to realise in a vague way that something terrible has happened but who isn't old enough to understand what it is, watches her mother's grief in silent astonishment. Mother has always stood for everything in the way of protection and power to the little one and now mother doesn't seem to be able to do anything. And so the child wanders off in a corner somewhere and doesn't even cry aloud, but in a subdued sort of way weeps itself asleep. The disciples "wist not what to answer him"—what could they say to comfort the Son of God, Himself? It is the inevitable penalty which a great soul must pay for its greatness, that by virtue of being above others it is cut off from the consolation of their sympathy. The disciples could have understood and comforted one of their own number, but they could not comfort the Christ.

And yet, if they had been able to have kept awake, which was all that Christ asked of them, how much better they would have been prepared for the ordeal which awaited them! There is a lesson in this fact for us to-day, the lesson that the mere effort to comfort, the effort to render service in any form is the best possible preparation for temptation and trial. How often do we say that we can do nothing for this or the other

[49]

person, and therefore it is useless to attempt anything. Peter felt that he could not help the Christ, but with a little extra effort he could have kept awake and watched with him. If he had done no more than this, doubtless in his own turn he would have gained strength sufficient to have kept him from denying his Master, a few hours later.

III. *The Prayers in Gethsemane.*

The great lesson of Gethsemane after all is contained in the prayers uttered by the Christ. Frederick W. Robertson was so impressed by the significance of these petitions that he based his entire philosophy of prayer upon them. Doubtless, this is an extreme view of the subject, for there are other prayers mentioned in the Bible which must be taken into account in order to secure a well-rounded viewpoint, and yet this position is not without justification.

The first petition is the expression of human weakness which finds a responsive chord in every soul that enters Gethsemane. "Oh my Father if it be possible let this cup pass from me. Nevertheless, not as I will, but as thou wilt." Jesus knew that all things were possible with God; why then could not this last bitter cup be taken away without the destruction of the Messiah's mission to the world? Had he not suffered enough as it was? Homeless and friendless, without a place to lay his head, patient in season and out of season, despised and rejected of men, why might he not have been spared the last awful agony of the cross?

Had it indeed been possible, there is no doubt but that his petition would have been granted.

How impossible it was, after the lapse of two thousand years, we can readily recognise. Without Calvary and the resurrection morn, Christianity would have been forgotten a few decades after the death of its founder. The last bitter cup was all-important in the programme of redemption. It set the seal upon the work of the Nazarene and enabled him to utter those sublime words "It is finished," when nailed to the cross.

There is a story, which is tolerably well authenticated, to the effect that a French philosopher, who lived in the days of the Revolution, devised what he thought was a perfect outline of a new religion, one that would supersede the old and outworn Christianity. He went to the Premier of France, who had no special reputation for piety, and presented the outline to him. The worldly-wise politician read it and then turned to the author and said, "There is only one thing it lacks in order that it may equal Christianity. That thing is that its author should submit to be scourged, beaten and crucified, and after having been buried for three days should raise himself from the dead. If if you can accomplish this, your religion will be worth something."

Jesus, himself, recognised the necessity for the cross in the second portion of his prayer. There is a wonderful consolation to us in our moments of weakness in the thought that even the Christ shrank from the cross. Fourteen hundred years after the crucifixion, in the market square of Rouen, a nineteen-year-old peasant girl was burned alive by a frantic mob of English soldiers. When they led her to the funeral pyre, she shrank from the flames and cried for water. But soon, the moment of weakness was over; the Christ who had passed through Gethsemane before her threw open the gates of Paradise to her eyes, and with one rapturous cry—"Jesus"—she passed to her reward. The church, under whose auspices she was burned, has since made her a saint and has placed her name in the calendar. But for us, the lesson of her life is the lesson of Gethsemane, the struggle between the flesh and the spirit, and the triumph granted to her in the end.

"Nevertheless, not as I will but as thou wilt." Between the first prayer and the second, the victory is already gained. The cry of Jesus is no longer "Let this cup pass," but rather "Thy will be done." Before His eyes, gifted with prophetic vision, rose a picture of the events of the morrow. He saw the trial before Pilate, the angry mob surging around him and crying "Crucify him! Crucify him!" He felt the crown of thorns sink into his brow. He watched the long procession take its way toward Calvary. He felt the nails pierce his hands and feet. He saw his mother weeping at the foot of the cross. But his spirit no longer shrank from the ordeal, for he had fought and won the battle in Gethsemane.

The third prayer in the garden is but a repetition of the second, uttered rather as a thanksgiving than a petition. He comes back to the sleeping disciples and tells them to sleep on for the hour when he needed their sympathy is over. Judas is already at hand and the Son of man is betrayed into hands of sinners.

IV. *The Practical Message of Gethsemane.*

In our daily struggles upward, struggles which after all are insignificant when compared with those of our Master, how we shrink day after day from the unpleasant duty which lies before us; how we hate to face it; how we use every means in our power to escape from it; how the spirit struggles with the flesh! And alas, too, how often with us the flesh gains the victory! This is the final lesson which I wish to draw from Gethsemane. Not all of us pass through it like the Christ. When we look ahead and see the bitter mockings of human tongues, and human criticisms, which await our action on the morrow; when we see the crown of thorns before us instead of the crown of laurel which our hearts had desired; when we feel the nails piercing through our hands and feet, as we are raised aloft on the cross of pain, our humiliation, or sacrifice, we flee from the vision; we abjure our hopes of the future; and our prayer is not "Lord, not as I will, but as thou wilt," but rather, "Lord, I will not have it so. I cannot bear it, there is no heaven for me!" And, if that be our prayer, there is no heaven for us. "To him that overcometh, to him will I give to drink of the fountain of life freely"—yes, always to him that overcometh. In that hour, human help will not avail, friends will have forsaken us, those

[53]

we have trusted will have proven broken reeds of comfort; only the Christ who passed through the garden can bring us strength and victory.

But in the hour of trial, let us not forget what victory means. Assuredly, it carries with it the new Eden, the Celestial Paradise, the Garden of God, the Tree of Life, the Throne of the Lamb, a residence forever in that place where there shall be no more pain, neither sorrow nor crying, and where God shall wipe away all tears from our eyes. It is the road to this land which lies through the garden of Gethsemane, and the only prayer that will enable us to pass through the garden is the supreme prayer of all the ages, "Father, not as I will, but as thou wilt." May that be the prayer of our hearts to-day, and always until the crown is won!

V

PASSION WEEK STUDIES

2: *Lessons from the Life of Judas*

TEXT: *Matthew* 10:4. "Judas Iscariot, who also betrayed him."

HUMANITY is strange, varied, inexplicable; both in its lights and in its shadows. Day is followed quickly by night: pleasure alternates with pain; sorrow is ever the companion of joy. There is a death's head at every feast, and if the bride wearing her orange blossoms were gifted with prophetic insight, she would see a grinning skeleton, peering with laughing mockery over her shoulder. Abel has Cain for a brother; Noah, Ham for a son; Christ, Judas for a disciple.

I. *Judas in Art.*

No character in the Bible save that of our Lord himself has provoked more serious discussion than Judas. He has found a place in art, in history and in literature; no less than in theology. One of the most striking characters in the realm of painting is that of Judas Iscariot. The earlier masters have all tried their hands on him. Giotto, the first of the great painters of the Rennaissance makes him a hideous, thick lipped, closely cropped monster; hardly a man at all. When we look at this portraiture, we wonder how Christ could ever have chosen such a creature, in the first place, as one of the Twelve.

In the city of Basle in Switzerland, there is a picture of the Last Supper, in which Judas is made so hideous that he becomes the central figure, obscuring in interest even the Christ. The painting is the work of Holbein, the great German artist. Judas Iscariot, it should be said, is never painted anywhere by himself. So intense was the hatred with which he was regarded during the Middle Ages that no picture with Judas alone in it would have survived the rage of the multitude over night. Hence we see him always with other figures; usually in the Last Supper, or in the betrayal. In the two most famous "Last Suppers" in the world, Leonardo da Vinci's in Milan, and Andrea del Sarto's in Florence, Judas is given a more noble appearance. Leonardo discloses him clutching the money bag tightly in his hand, and at the same time overturning the salt-cellar in his excitement, or fright. The stamp of villainy is upon his countenance, but the face is not hideous in itself; in fact, it is rather handsome, so far as the individual features are concerned. Andrea has pictured the traitor as a miserable, weak, specimen of humanity exciting our pity, if anything, more than our disgust.

A peculiar characteristic of all the paintings in which Judas appears is the color of the clothing which he wears. In every case, it is a dingy, dirty yellow. It is said to be on this account that yellow is so universally disliked in Spain and Italy. Malefactors sentenced to the scaffold or to the stake, galley slaves and the like, in these countries, were always clad in yellow. In Venice for a long time the Jews were obliged by law to wear yellow hats, and the feeling has come down in our own day in such slang phrases as "yellow journalism," or "playing yellow" in football, or other athletic sports. In some of the earlier pictures, the entrance of Satan into Judas is pictured by a little black demon, which is seen seated on his shoulder, whispering to him, or even entering his mouth.

II. *Judas in Legend.*

But not only in the realm of art has imagination been busy with the character of the arch-traitor of the universe. Legends concerning his history were numerous in the Middle Ages filling in all the details which the gospel narratives omitted. It was said that even before his birth it had been prophesied that he should kill his own parents and betray his God. Terrified by the vision, his father had him enclosed in a chest and cast into the sea. The waters bore him to a strange country, where he was picked up by the king and queen and adopted as their son. When he grew up, his malignant nature soon made itself manifest. He oppressed and finally killed his brother, the real son of the king, and then fled to Judea and entered the service of Pontius Pilate as a page. Afterwards, in accordance with the prediction, he killed his parents, and then overcome by a momentary remorse, he entered the service of Jesus of Nazareth. Avarice, the one sin of which he had not previously been guilty, now took possession of him, and under its spell he betrayed his master.

It is needless to say that this old tradition, which was pretty universally believed during the Middle Ages, has no foundation in fact. The early church historians, on the contrary, attribute no inherent malignancy to Judas. Eusebius, one of the greatest of them all, says "Christ gave like gifts to Judas with the other apostles, and once our Saviour had good hopes of him, on account of the power of the free will, for Judas was not of such nature as rendered his salvation impossible; like the other apostles he might have been instructed by the Son of God, and might have been a sincere and good disciple."

Samuel Taylor Coleridge, the great English poet and essayist, took exactly the opposite view to the one expressed by Eusebius, but used it as the basis of an elaborate apology for the traitor. According to Coleridge, Christ must have been betrayed, and Judas was the one who was destined to betray him, hence no fault in the man himself attached to his action. Modern writers, like Paul Heyse, in Germany, in his famous production, "Mary of Magdala," have sometimes ennobled Judas. Heyse, makes him one of the central figures of the drama, and motives his actions by considerations of disappointed ambition and love. Judas had lost faith in Christ because of the failure of the latter to establish a great earthly kingdom and to drive

the hated Romans out of Palestine. A mistaken patriotism thus helped to explain the enormity of his
crime. It may be worth while to add to the other
opinions the universal belief of the followers of Mohammed, who have a strange superstition that Christ
was caught up to heaven, and Judas, in his likeness,
was crucified in his place.

III. *Judas in the Gospel Narrative.*

Out of this jumble of legendary material and fantastic speculation it is an infinite relief to turn to the
pages of the Gospels and to read the simple story of the
life of Judas just as they have given it. No more facts
than they contain are needed in order to understand
his character. A few strokes of the pencil give us,
as if by magic, a complete outline of his history.

Something, at least, hints at the predominating characteristic of his life in the lurid sketch of avarice revealed by his comment upon the anointing of Christ in
the house of Mary and Martha. John, who was one of
the Twelve, and knew the character of Judas well,
says of him in plain words that he was a thief and a
hypocrite into the bargain.

Our interest in Judas in this study, however, deals
primarily with the last day of his life. When we think
of what that last day stands for, we usually waste little
time on Judas. Our interest in him begins and ends
in the betrayal scene; after that he fades from our
view. And yet that last day was as much a tragedy
for Judas as it was for the Master he betrayed. Let
us sketch briefly the outlines of the tragedy.

IV. *The Tragedy of Judas.*

There are four scenes following each other in rapid succession which tell the story of the tragedy of Judas. In the first scene, he is seated around the table with the other disciples partaking of the Last Supper. Strange black thoughts fill his heart. He has not been honest in his dealings, and he knows the one whom he serves well enough to know that this fact is not hidden from him. He feels condemned in the presence of his Master's purity. Moreover, may he not be called to a reckoning, and then what will happen? A disgraceful discharge from the band with the brand of "thief" written across his brow. In this frame of mind, he is quite ready to bring excuses to his conscience for the villainy he meditates. We can imagine his soliloquy as he thinks over the situation:

He begins by casting doubts upon the Messiahship of his Master. "Had he been the Christ," he says to himself, "he would have restored, long ere this, the power and the glory of the temple of Jehovah to Jerusalem. When the people wanted to make him a king, he timidly refused to accept their leadership. He played the coward when he ought to have played the hero. He, the Messiah, here in this little room, hiding in obscurity from the High Priest and the elders of his people! Not such was the Messiah of Israel promised to be. Moreover, he is sure, sooner or later, to be taken; whether I betray him or not. The High Priest and the authorities have soldiers and spies everywhere; it is only a question of a day sooner or a day later, and I had as well have the money as any one else. Then after they have arrested him, what will they do with him? Probably beat him, and discipline him and let him go. They cannot put him to death, for it is against the law so to do."

I do not think that Judas ever for a moment faced the thought of the crucifixion of Christ before he betrayed him. His after-remorse furnishes strong ground for this opinion. Moreover, I do not think that any human being, if he could have foreseen all that took place afterward could have deliberately betrayed him. Judas was deceived, like most other criminals. He bargained for more than he intended.

While these things are passing through the mind of Judas, the calm eyes of the Master gifted with more than mortal insight are reading, as in a book, every fleeting thought of his soul. Suddenly, he glances up with fixed determination written in his face; the final motive has appeared which will determine his will. What is it? It is the final motive always in the life of the thief. Gold! "I shall have gold!" A paltry sum, the bribe appears in our eyes, but to the avaricious, whether the amount be small or large, money always brings temptation. . . . The decision is made, with all its momentous consequences for the future. Judas looks up and his gaze meets the sad face of the Christ. The latter knows, too, what the decision is. With him there is a natural desire to be alone with those who have remained faithful; a desire likewise that the dreadful events which are to follow shall take place as soon as possible. "That thou doest, do quickly," he says, in strange warning notes to the traitor. Judas, his purposes kindled to a brighter blaze by the realisation that they are known, goes out, and the evangelist adds, with a wonderfully lurid touch, "when he went out it was night." Yes, night for Judas for evermore. Night with its black wings of despair hovering over his soul, black, hideous, unending night! Young man on the downward pathway; sometime you will leave the lights of the upper chambers of the Good, and as you slam the doors of Innocence and Purity upon your soul, you will plunge out into the night alone. Beware, lest on your pathway, phantoms like those which pursued the Iscariot dog your heels! Terrible words are those: "he went out and it was night."

V. *The Second Scene in the Tragedy.*

The second scene occurs in a lonely garden without the walls of the city. Judas has bargained with High Priest. The money has been paid him. It jingles in the pocket of his girdle. There are strange misgivings in his soul, but the music of the coin in his purse drowns them all.

The crafty Caiaphas will have his victim before the traitor repents of his choice. A guard is ready immediately. Judas knows where to take them. Silently, hurriedly, they thread their way through the crowded streets of the capital. Then they come to the brook Cedron; stream immortal in the history of the world. As they pass over and enter the garden, suddenly, out of the shades, a figure presents himself saying, "Whom seek you?" The guards fall back in astonishment, but Judas, eager to earn his money, steps forward and says in hollow tones, "Hail, Master!" and kisses him. Then the Master looks at him with that gaze which never left the eyes of Judas until they were closed in the quietude of death. "Judas," he says, "betrayest thou the Son of man with a kiss?" "Will you," in other words, "make the symbol of your previous devotion the means of betraying the best friend you have?"

There was no time for Judas to reply, if he could have replied. Simon Peter has attacked the servant of the High Priest and wounded him. In the confusion, the disciples have fled, one and all; Jesus having forbidden them to use any means of defence. Judas slinks away from the band as they bear their prisoner off to the temple court for his first trial before Annas. Somehow, the jingle of the money in his pocket is not as attractive as it had been. Those words "Betrayest thou the Son of man with a kiss?" keep ringing in his ears. He cannot get away from them. Like a murderer, who, after his crime has been committed, hopes against hope that his victim will come back to life, Judas hopes that his Master may soon be released. Nevertheless a dreadful foreboding is in his heart. He roams over the city seeking rest and finding none. The jingle of the money has become almost hateful; it has lost all of its attraction. Daylight dawns and suddenly he finds himself before the hall of the Roman governor. There is a great tumult; an immense crowd of people are crying out, "Crucify him, Crucify him!" Judas pushes closer through the crowd. He climbs up where he can look over the shoulders of those in front of him, and then he sees his Master crowned with thorns, the blood streaming down his face, and ready to be led away to the cross!

VI. *The Third Scene in the Tragedy.*

Judas slips back into the crowd, and as he does so, the money jingles again in his girdle. He hears again the words "betrayest thou the Son of man with a kiss?" His mind is a chaos of wild, indistinct thoughts. Only one thing seems clear to him—he must get rid of that money. He hastens through the struggling mass of humanity about him. He seeks everywhere for the High Priest. At last he finds him. He appeals to the crafty Sadducee, who only laughs at him now that he has served his term. "I have sinned in that I have betrayed the innocent blood," he says in harsh tones of despair. Again the Sadducee laughs: "What is that to us?" he says, "see thou to that."

Modern prodigal, in the courts of sin; allured by specious promises of those who would have you forsake the path of goodness; ruined, betrayed, undone at last, what have those for whom you have sacrificed body and soul to tell you as your final reward? Always the same mocking words, "What is that to us? see thou to that!" In all the awful vocabulary of perdition, there is no language so terribly bitter, so poignant, so infused with the very incarnation of wretchedness and despair as those words of the High

Priest to Judas. And now what shall Judas do, when he realizes their meaning? Alas for the miserable victim of sin. He has cast off by his own action the friendship of the Good, and now the friends he has bought at the cost of his own soul, forsake him and mock him. No one in all the wide world is so utterly alone. It is perhaps the final curse of perdition that it destroys all fellowship and condemns its votaries to the terrible solitude of their own guilty souls.

VII. *The Last Scene.*

For Judas there can be but one end. Had the Gospel narrative said nothing about it, we could have easily surmised the truth. Only one road is left open to him. The cold, desolate road of the suicide. Wildly, madly, he throws down the money which had lured him to his doom, in front of the High Priest. Hardly knowing where he is going, he rushes blindly through the streets;—anywhere, just so he can get away from that last scene in the Garden. He passes by deserted houses; the inhabitants are out to witness some spectacle, his mind surmises what it is—he has seen people crucified before. He hurries on until he gets beyond the walls. Then as he turns to the deserted edge of Hinnom, over whose precipitous rocky walls the brain becomes dizzy as one looks down, for a moment he seems at rest. There is no soul near, only the clear Judean sky above, only the warm, clear sunlight bathing his feet.

He has almost forgotten that he is Judas, when suddenly he hears strange sounds from another section of the walls. He stops and listens. Again and again the tumultuous cry goes up. He knows what it is. It is the procession beginning its march to Golgotha. . . .

Over the grave of Judas in the potter's field, the Angel of Eternity has inscribed this epitaph: "The wages of sin is death."

VI

3: *The Greater Sin*

TEXT: *John* 19:11. "Therefore he that delivered me unto thee hath the greater sin."

THE text fixes special responsibility upon a particular individual. It asserts that one above others is chargeable with peculiar guilt in the crucifixion of Jesus of Nazareth. Perhaps to most people the name of the individual specified comes as a surprise. If the suffrage of the world and particularly of the past ages were taken I suppose that the Iscariot would easily lead in the infamous competition. For ages, Judas has been regarded as the worst man that ever lived. When Dante wrote his Inferno, he put Judas down at the very bottom of perdition. When Robert Browning wanted somebody to associate on terms of equality with the worst character he could imagine, he picked Judas Iscariot. The Devil himself was not more cordially detested during the Middle Ages than was the traitor of the Twelve. The Devil with his horns and hoofs was expected to be bad—it was his nature— but Judas had no such excuse.

Ranking next to Judas in the competition, according to popular estimation, came the man who sentenced

Jesus to the cross—the Roman Governor Pilate. People could not forget that but for Pilate's sentence Jesus would have escaped the awful death before him. Pilate had it in his power to save or to condemn, and he condemned; against his own will, perhaps, but the sentence none the less deadly on that account. The Crusaders before the walls of Jerusalem heaped their maledictions upon the head of Pontius Pilate. His name, like that of Judas, is in bad odour even to-day and he has had few namesakes, to say the least in Christian lands.

I. *The Man Who Had the Greater Sin.*

And yet the New Testament narrative, if carefully studied, shows that there was at least one man who was more guilty than either Judas or Pilate. There was one who lured the wretched traitor to his doom; who offered the money and when the deal was closed, and Judas repented of his bargain, laughed with cold-blooded indifference in his face. There was one who persuaded and threatened the unwilling Roman Governor until he passed sentence upon the victim of Judas. There was one who in defiance of law wrung an unjust sentence from the Sanhedrin and whose sleepless enmity fired the mob to cry out, "Away with him! Crucify him! Crucify him!" The words of Jesus himself, as recorded in the text, fix the deepest stigma of guilt upon this man's brow. When Pilate in a species of insolent bravado said to him, "Speakest thou not unto me? knowest thou not that I have power to crucify thee and power to release thee?" Jesus replied, with the calm dignity of the martyr, "Thou couldst have no power at all against me except it were given thee from above: therefore he that delivered me unto thee hath the greater sin."

The man to whom he referred was named Joseph Caiaphas, for eleven years High Priest of the Jewish people, and to whose charge more than to that of any other one man in the world must be laid the crime of Calvary.

II. *The Trials of Jesus.*

There are three stages in the story which begins at Gethsemane and which ends on Golgotha. Over the first, like some malignant comet, the star of Judas rules; over the second, that of Caiaphas; and over the third, that of Pilate. When Judas' trembling lips pronounced the words "Hail Master!" and kissed him, his part in his Master's tragedy was over. His work had been done. While the temple mob with their lanterns and swords and staves are hurrying Jesus off to the palace of Annas, the father-in-law of Caiaphas, Judas slips away. From about one o'clock in the morning until day-break Jesus is in the hands of Caiaphas; after that he is in charge of Pilate. During these four or five hours he is tried three times. First by Annas, the former High Priest and predecessor of Caiaphas who is unable to extract anything of value from him. Annas, therefore, sends him bound to Caiaphas where he has his second trial before a picked group of hostile members of the Sanhedrin, illegally assembled, by whom he is found guilty, with the most flagrant violation of law, and sentenced to death. After daylight has dawned, in order to give a semblance of formality to the sentence, Caiaphas hastily assembles the full Sanhedrin and obtains its sanction for the sentence which the earlier group had pronounced.

In all, Jesus appears to have had seven distinct trials: the first before Annas; the second and third before Caiaphas; the fourth before Pilate; the fifth before Herod Antipas; and the sixth and seventh before Pilate. Never was there a man in this world, before or since, tried so often in so short a time, and yet, after all of his trials, condemned with so little pretence of justice.

With the man who was the chief agent in the first three trials we have to do in the present study. If I were expressing my own opinion of the relative guilt of those who had a hand in the death of Jesus, I would put Caiaphas first, then Annas, then the Chief Priests who were his companions, then Herod Antipas, then Judas, and Pilate last. This arrangement has been suggested by some careful students of the history, and it would seem to approach very closely to the truth.

III. *The Trial before Annas.*

Annas, before whom Jesus was taken first, is a character often mentioned in the history of the times outside of the gospels. He had been High Priest himself for five or six years and no less than five of his sons, a son-in-law and a grandson had filled or were to fill that position. Annas, according to history, was avaricious and fond of luxury and ease. He and his family enjoyed a monopoly on the illegal sale of articles in the temple courts which had been so severely condemned by Jesus when he drove the money changers out of the temple with whips of cord. Business reasons no less than other considerations had therefore whetted his hatred of the Galilean prophet. He differs, at least as we see him in the gospels from his son-in-law in the fact that he is more crafty and less openly severe and unjust in his proceedings. Christ was doubtless taken before him first in order that his skilful powers of cross-examination might secure some evidence to be used at the later trial.

The account of the trial before Annas is given only in the Gospel of John. The priestly examiner asked questions which related to two specific objects: the nature of Christ's teaching, and the names of his followers. To both queries, he received answers entirely unsatisfactory, and he was obliged to send his prisoner to Caiaphas without having secured any evidence. The man who had outwitted the most skilful followers of Annas in the temple on the Tuesday before, had no difficulty in foiling their master. So ended the preliminary trial before Annas.

IV. *The Trials before Caiaphas.*

The first trial before Caiaphas gives us a full length portrait of the man. Only a few weeks before, just

after the raising of Lazarus, he had declared that
Jesus must die for the good of the people, an uncon-
scious prophecy to be fulfilled in quite the opposite
sense to that in which he intended. He meant that if
this man kept on teaching, the house of Caiaphas and
the Jewish hierarchy were doomed; it was therefore
expedient that the man should be gotten out of the road.
Caiaphas had been back of the bitter hatred of the
Jerusalem Jews toward Jesus throughout the preced-
ing year, he had used every means to apprehend the
Nazarene but did not dare attempt it openly for fear of
the people. Now, unexpectedly, the treason of Judas
plays into his hands. Hastily gathering together some
of his associates upon whom he can rely most assuredly,
he summons them to his palace. It is probably between
one and two in the morning, an illegal hour for the
Sanhedrin to meet. Jesus is brought before them from
the examination before Annas just on the other side
of the temple square. There is no legal evidence
against the prisoner, but this fact does not disturb
Caiaphas. He has two witnesses hastily summoned,
but in his hurry they have been badly coached and at
once contradict each other. Then he resorts to the expedient of extorting from the prisoner himself the
confession which will seal his doom. With spectacular
pretence he steps down from his seat as judge, and
taking the place as prosecutor demands of Jesus
whether he is or is not the Christ, "the Son of the
Blessed." As soon as the Nazarene has answered in
the affirmative, he has him declared guilty and adjourns
the meeting. Then when the sun has dawned, he calls

a formal assembly of the Sanhedrin and secures a technical endorsement of the earlier meeting.

After this third formal trial, he sends his prisoner on to Pilate, the Roman Governor, with a request that he be put to death, and the burden of responsibility is shifted, in part at least, to the shoulders of the Roman.

V. *The Character of Caiaphas.*

When we come to a careful study of Caiaphas himself, we find the whole story revealed by his actions in three momentous crises of his history. The first occurs when, after his question to Jesus, he steps back and with dramatic emphasis tears his robe from one end to the other, as though the answer of the Galilean was too horrible to be believed. Here the arrant hypocrisy of the man comes into play. The second incident takes place before the judgment hall of Pilate early on the morning of Friday, the day of the crucifixion. The Sanhedrin officials have brought Jesus, with the sentence of death, to Pilate in order that he may be executed. With murder in their hearts and the stain of innocent blood on their hands, they nevertheless refuse to enter the Governor's hall for fear of being ceremonially defiled. John tells the story: "And it was early, and they themselves went not into the judgment hall lest they should be defiled; but that they might eat the passover." Here we have a splendid example of that terrible formalism which Jesus had condemned so often before. It was to this sort of thing that he referred when he said: "Ye blind guides, which strain at a gnat, and swallow a camel." The third incident occurred at the crucial moment when Pilate brings Jesus for the last time before the multitude and says: "Behold your King." With the blood-stained brow of the innocent man, weak and faint as he was from scourging, before them Pilate rightly counted on a revulsion of feeling on the part of the people. But Caiaphas is equal to the emergency: He has the word passed around to all of his followers to set up a great cry—"We have no king but Cæsar." . . .

How sardonically Pilate must have smiled when he heard such a slogan from the lips of people who hated Cæsar and the Roman rule worse than they hated Apollyon himself. Caiaphas and the Jews, Cæsar's friends! Very proud Cæsar would be of their friendship too, if he knew it! But the trick works; Pilate dared not resist such an appeal, and Caiaphas, by an infamous deception, succeeds at last in condemning an innocent man to the cross.

VI. *Caiaphas as a Jew.*

In the character of Caiaphas we see as in a mirror the worst traits of his people focussed together and personified. The Jews have been, and are to-day, a peculiar people. The have furnished some of the best material that history knows, and they have likewise furnished some of the worst. They produced in olden times, Ahab and Abraham, Judas and Joshua, Caiaphas and Christ. Read the literature of the world and you find the same contrast. Scott's greatest heroine is a

Jewess; Dickens' worst character is a Jew. Shakespeare's Shylock is so difficult to interpret that we hardly know where to class him, while Marlowe's Barabas is the most thoroughly bloodthirsty villain that humanity has ever imagined.

It is a strange fact that the most striking characteristics of a people or of an age are often exhibited in some one individual. In this way, one man may stand for a whole generation, or a whole epoch. Shakespeare sums up in himself a century of literary history—nay, more, he is probably the typical Anglo-Saxon of all time. Goethe, with his profundity of thought, his many-sidedness, his insatiable curiosity, is the typical German, and will doubtless always remain so. Dante stands for Italy and the Middle Ages; Lincoln represents America, and Napoleon, France. In these people, the genius of the age somehow became incarnate, and hence to know them means to know in large measure those for whom they stand.

In his wonderful criticism of that most celebrated of all portraits, the Mona Lisa in Paris, Mr. Walter Pater argues that in this one woman the artist has embodied the history of her sex from the days of Eve down to the present age. He sees in her reflections of the coquetry of Helen of Troy, of the wiles of Cleopatra of the Nile, of the beautiful devotion of Saint Anne—in short, she is the embodiment of the entire history of womanhood. It is an idea akin to this which I find necessary in the solution of the character of Caiaphas. The man himself is only the final and complete incarnation of the worst traits of that nation whose wilfulness had so often led it to destruction, and whose rebellious disposition was doomed to bring down a still more awful vengeance upon its head. The blood-thirsty Ahab, the cruel and idolatrous Manasseh, the mad freaks of Saul, the tyranny of Rehoboam all ran in the blood and coursed through the veins of Caiaphas. Not even the Son of God himself could save such a man from destruction.

In the parable of the Wicked Husbandmen, Jesus had illustrated the impossibility of averting destruction from his people. The Master of the Vineyard had sent his messengers time and again to the husbandmen, but they had beaten them and sent them away empty. Last of all, he sent his beloved Son, saying, "Surely they will respect him." But the husbandmen killed him, and cast him out of the vineyard with the callous comment: "He is the heir and the inheritance shall be ours." So thought Caiaphas and his followers when they counselled that one man should die for the people. In the end, however, the Master destroys the wicked husbandmen and lets the vineyard out to others. In like manner, forty years after the crucifixion of Jesus, Jerusalem is besieged and destroyed by Titus; the Jewish nation is dispersed; the temple is burned, never to be rebuilt, and the family of Caiaphas disappears from the face of the earth.

VII. *Final Lessons.*

The life of Caiaphas is strangely different from the life of Judas, or the life of Pilate. No repentance, or regret tinges the story of his career. In his descent into the final and bottomless pit of infamy he has no place left for conscience or remorse. A cold, callous, calculative hatred is his natural atmosphere, and for him there is no hope of repentance, since his own nature cannot understand the term. As we study his life, the fiery denunciations of the twenty-third chapter of Matthew become clear and luminous. Blood-thirsty, hypocritical to the core, externally religious, avaricious, and blinded by the lust for power and gold, he stands before the world as a type of the level to which humanity is capable of sinking, and a living proof of the hideous implications of the problem of evil. Why the world should want to create an artificial Devil when it has produced such characters as Caiaphas, and a few others of the same class, is beyond calculation. He appears to come nearest of all historic figures to that incarnation of evil which Shakespeare drew so perfectly in Iago. But Caiaphas is compacted of flesh and blood, while Iago is not. He has his lesson, too, for us. In the rogues' galleries of the world are many faces which were once the opposite of what they appear in the gallery. There is the possibility of Caiaphas in all of us. We can sin against the Spirit of Light until our hearts become so hardened that even conscience dies and with it all hope of pardon.

There are characters like Coleridge's "Life in Death" which wear the mask of humanity, but which "thick man's blood with cold," for they are dead to all chance of moral resurrection. To such a class we must assign the man who plotted and brought about the crucifixion of Jesus. We dare not use harsh terms when we speak of him, for his nature freezes us into silence. We dare not pity, attack, or condemn. We can only look into his face as we look into the black waters of some treacherous subterranean abyss whose unknown depths stir us with horror and aversion. And the most terrible comment we can make is to say, as we pass on with a shudder, "This being was once too, a man!"

VII

(*An Easter Sermon*)

TEXT: *Job* 14:14. "If a man die, shall he live again?"

SOME one has said that the great problems of the universe are all embodied in three simple questions: "Whence came I? What am I? and whither am I going?" These questions are all, more or less interwoven, and the answer to one is necessarily the key to the answer to the others. No man has stood by the bedside of a friend and watched the life slowly ebb away until at last the form which was once bubbling over with animation and gaiety has become a clod more repulsive even than its companion clods of earth, without asking the question of Job, "If a man die, shall he live again?"

No man, too, has seen the casket lowered into the ground and pronounced, or heard pronounced, the solemn words; "Earth to earth; dust to dust; ashes to ashes," without asking himself how far those words are true, and what is the exact significance they ought to convey. Aside from any question of religious belief, these questions force themselves upon us, and he would be callous to an unmeasured degree who did not give them some consideration. Doubtless, with most of us,

[79]

there is always a tendency, even in spite of ourselves, to take what we are sure of and let the rest alone. This tendency is embodied in the old proverb to the effect that a bird "in the hand is worth two in the bush," or as Robert Herrick puts it:

> "Gather ye rosebuds while ye may
> Old Time is still a flying."

or, in the quatrains of an Omar:

> "Some for the Glories of this world, and some
> Sigh for the Prophet's Paradise to come.
> Ah, take the Cash and let the Credit go
> Nor heed the rumble of a distant drum;
>
> Oh, threats of Hell and hopes of Paradise!
> One thing at least is certain: this life flies.
> One thing is certain and the rest is lies,
> The Flower that once has blown forever dies."

I. *The Philosophy of Materialism.*

On one of the oldest mausoleums discovered in the East is the inscription, comprising the epitaph of one of the greatest monarchs of the ancient time, "Let us eat, drink, and be merry, for the rest is nothing." And so materialism, or the belief that the body, or matter, is the only reality is very old and has always had numerous advocates. Some of the Old Testament writers, like the author of Ecclesiastes and even the authors of certain of the psalms, seem to look upon the body as an essential condition of existence. The ancient Egyptians embalmed their dead because they believed they would need their bodies when they were raised for judgment. Even the early Christians were, for the most part, materialists, as the clause in the Apostle's Creed relating to the resurrection of the flesh indicates, and while they universally held to the miracle of the ultimate resurrection of the body, they nevertheless believed that there could be no life without it. Saint Paul combated this theory in the fifteenth chapter of First Corinthians.

Coming on down the ages to the present era, materialism has held its own, and during the last century it gained tremendous influence through the advances of modern science. Researches in biology, and the closer study of other departments of life have shown the intimate connection between the body and the soul, and have led many people to believe that the less obvious one is only the product of the other.

II. *The Arguments for Materialism.*

Various arguments have been advanced to prove this position. It has been shown by experiment that mental diseases are always accompanied by disorder of brain tissue; that the pressure of a slight piece of the skull upon the brain will cause insanity, and that the insanity will disappear when the operation known as trepanning, is performed. There are hospital cases on record where operations affected even the moral nature of the patient and transformed an incorrigible, vicious child into a docile and obedient boy. It has been shown that certain sections of the brain govern certain fields of thinking and action, and that the two things, if not causally related, at least run side by side. The ma-

[81]

terialist points proudly to the fact that no mind or soul has ever been known without a brain, and that size and fineness of brain structure have always gone hand in hand with genius and intellectual development. There is a certain limit of brain size below which the person possessing it is sure to be an idiot. Most great men have had large brains, though it is acknowledged that there have been exceptions to the rule.

Moreover, the general dependence of the mind upon the body is elaborated at length. A person cannot do prolonged mental labour without physical nourishment. When the body is fatigued the mind is not at its best; when the stomach is out of order, the person has the blues; when the nerves are diseased, he is fussy and irritable and takes an erratic view of life. If Thomas Carlyle had not been a confirmed dyspeptic, who knows whether he would have been so melancholy in temperament? Who shall say that Browning's optimism was not in part due to a healthy liver and to an unrivaled digestive system? If Schopenhauer had not been diseased in body and brain he might never have been a pessimist; and the crazy philosophy of Nietzsche, which has wrought so much harm in the world may be best accounted for by serious lesions of the brain, I am inclined to think not only on the part of the philosopher but also of his adherents. "Let a man work hard," says the materialist, "and get but little to eat and he soon becomes a full-fledged pessimist, while if you give him capon and terrapin and a good digestive system he is apt to take a tolerant if not indeed a roseate view of his surroundings.

There is a further argument drawn from the effect of age and disease upon the brain and its corresponding influence upon the mind. As a man grows older and weaker in body, his mind becomes less vigorous; the memory fails along with the nerves, and the power of quick and ready thought is not as acute as it was in the earlier years of his life.

It would not seem to be necessary, however, to state at further length the position of those who hold that the body, or the material existence, is the real man or the real woman. Let it suffice to say that if the influence of the mind upon the body be of great importance, as is frequently asserted, no less strong and cogent arguments can be brought to prove a like influence of the body upon the mind. Human life, on the surface at least, is a dualism and it depends largely upon the point of view we choose as to which side we shall see. Materialism, it is unnecessary to say, is the easy and obvious solution of the world. If we can imagine a cow or a horse thinking over the question at all, it is the philosophy which either or both of them would choose. It is the philosophy of the present moment and its teachings are easy to hold and to understand. There has always been a great deal of it in the world, and while men remain partly animal in their structure, as they are, it is only reasonable to suppose that there will be some who will elect to believe that they are wholly animal. There are poets of materialism like Whitman (though Whitman was not altogether a materialist), and prophets of materialism like Elbert Hubbard (though Hubbard was not altogether a prophet), and believers in materialism who defy the laws of society in so far as they place any restrictions upon the earthly side of their natures; and yet it is no less true that the moulders of the world's thought and the builders of the world's ideals never have been and never will be, materialists.

III. *The Case against Materialism.*

There was never a supremely great philosopher, poet or constructive genius of any kind who thought that the body was the all and all of life. Plato, Socrates, Kant, Homer, Shakespeare, Milton, Dante, Virgil, Goethe, Michael Angelo were all of them, idealists of an advanced type. "We feel that we are greater than we know," and though life begins in the dust we have a heritage which reaches to the stars. It is the unique privilege of man that he has thoughts "beyond the reaches of his soul," thoughts which "wander through eternity." Materialism not only cuts us off from these but it curtails the proper enjoyment of its own legitimate pleasures. As the body reacts on the soul, so the soul reacts on the body, and the man or the woman who gives the soul its proper place in his or her life is apt to have the most harmonious and desirable bodily existence.

I knew a man, a bank president in my home town, who was a disbeliever in the immortality of the soul, and yet all of his life he was in mortal terror of dying and nearly drove himself frantic avoiding, or trying to avoid, disease, and dieting himself to prolong his

[84]

existence to the last possible minute. On the whole, I think he led the most miserable life of which I have had any knowledge. There are few even of the most confirmed materialists who are always quite sure of their position. They may confidently assert that death ends all, but how do they know? It is useless to chaff the man who believes in a future life by saying that when a man dies we know nothing more of the soul. Of course not, but by the same token we know nothing of its annihilation. The man talked to us an hour ago; he talks no more, but does that prove that he has vanished into nothingness? When he talked we did not see him, we saw his lips move but the lips were not the man and the question is where has the man gone?

Materialism, by its own discoveries, has in fact practically committed suicide. The discovery of the law of the Conservation of Energy, which Professor Huxley styled the greatest achievement of the nineteenth century, proves that although energy constantly changes form it is never destroyed. Heat goes into steam; steam into electricity, and so on, but no energy is ever lost. Now the highest possible form of energy is the human personality. At death, there is a change, that is certain, but does the change mean the destruction of personality? If it does, nature is here, at the most important position in her realm, contradicting herself and negating her own law. The human body is entirely renewed every seven years. Not a particle of fibre which was in my body seven years ago, in all probability, is in it to-day; and yet I was myself then and I am myself now. I have changed but I am still the same man. And so, when the last great change comes, does it mean that that change is to be annihilation or extinction? The man who so asserts takes a tremendous responsibility upon himself. Callous, indeed, must he be, if he does not inwardly repeat with Hamlet:

> "To die;—to sleep;—
> To sleep, perchance to dream;—ay, there's the rub;
> For in that sleep of death what dreams may come,
> When we have shuffled off this mortal coil,
> Must give us pause."

IV. *The Christian Solution.*

It is just here where we pause, in our earthly reasoning, that the divine answer comes. Of ourselves, we cannot solve the problem. There is nothing in nature which will absolutely demonstrate immortality, but there is just as certainly nothing which disproves it. Hence there arises both the necessity and the possibility of a revelation such as that which God has made through Jesus Christ: The necessity, because of ourselves we cannot solve the problem; the possibility, because there is nothing in nature to contradict the truthfulness of the solution. It is for this reason that the gospel of the resurrection has practically conquered the world. The Apostle Paul was right when he staked the whole case for the Christian religion upon the fact of the resurrection. If Christianity has made no contribution here, there is no chance that the religion of Christ will become the ultimate religion of humanity. It is the gospel of the Open Tomb which means most to the sorely tried and broken hearted of all the ages.

In the face of the Christian solution of the eternal question, the man who does not accept that solution has the option of standing before the open grave and in answer to the question of the text: "if a man die, shall he live again?" of saying, "I affirm of my own will that he shall not live." Prove it, he cannot; affirm it, he may. And what, pray, does he gain by the affirmation? The heritage of the beast of the field and the fowls of the air, instead of the heritage of the hero, the sage, or the martyr; the goal of the libertine, the drunkard, the man who has wasted and spoiled the goodly inheritance of eternity, and who would fain escape any reckoning by doing away at once with responsibility and with life; the portion of the coward and the slothful, the coveted boon of the idler and the debauchee.

Is it not an infinitely better choice to bravely affirm, in the light of revelation and with at least the full permission of reason: "I believe in a heritage beyond the stars; in a resurrection from the grave, and in an immortality of light; in a destiny worthy of him who was created in the image of God and who chooses never to renounce or to barter away his immortal birthright!"

VIII

(*Mother's Day Sermon*)

TEXT: The Magnificat, *Luke* 1:46-55.

"And Mary said, My soul doth magnify the Lord,
And my spirit hath rejoiced in God my Savior.
For he hath regarded the low estate of his handmaiden:
For, behold, from henceforth all generations shall call
　　me blessed
For he that is mighty hath done to me great things,
And holy is his name.
And his mercy is on them that fear him
From generation to generation.
He hath shewed strength with his arm;
He hath scattered the proud in the imagination of their
　　hearts.
He hath put down the mighty from their seats,
And exalted them of low degree.
He hath filled the hungry with good things;
And the rich he hath sent empty away.
He hath holpen his servant Israel,
In remembrance of his mercy;
As he spake to our fathers,
To Abraham, and to his seed for ever.

[88]

I. *The Woman of Leonardo.*

In that magnificent collection of paintings and statuary in the Louvre, which is the pride of Paris and the people of France, there is the portrait of a woman now somewhat faded with age and withal so simple and unostentatious in appearance that the average tourist, if left to himself, would probably pass it by unnoticed. When he is told, however, by his guide or his guide book, as the case may be, that this faded portrait is the greatest art treasure—unless the Venus de Milo be an exception—in the possession of the French people, he pauses to notice it more carefully. If he is a man of discernment, he will be conscious of a peculiar fascination gradually stealing over him as he gazes into the face of the woman who looks down from her canvas imprisonment of over four hundred years. The eyes seem to read the soul and to draw forth its secrets whether willingly released or not. There is the most bewitching of all smiles that have ever been imagined playing around the beautiful lips and mouth; the hair and the hands are perfect. Surely, we say, here was a woman born to command and to sway the hearts of men, and to lead them whithersoever she would. We go away from that room feeling impressed with the innate power which woman can wield as we have never felt it before. And yet there is an uncanny sensation also present of which we are conscious and from which we cannot escape. I do not believe that any one has ever left that room in the Louvre and wished for just such a woman for either a wife, a sister, a daughter or a mother. Nevertheless, she embodied the greatest conception in portraiture of the most daring genius in art—the world renowned Leonardo da Vinci.

We have been gazing, as many of you have doubtless guessed, upon the Mona Lisa of Leonardo—the final achievement in portraiture of the artist who painted what is usually regarded as the greatest picture in the world, the Last Supper, at Milan, and the painter whose conception of the Christ face is the only one in the realm of art which is at all worthy of its subject.

II. *The Woman of Raphael.*

But perhaps we do not have a great deal of time to spend in Paris, and so the train is soon whirling us across what were once the magnificent wheat-land and the vine-clad orchards of Burgundy and the Rhine, where the fields used to be like great gardens and where the roads were solid and level as marble so that one horse could draw as much as three can in this country, but a land which is now little more than a collection of shell-dug craters of earth and rock, until, in perhaps a few weeks, we arrive in Dresden, the capital of Saxony, and the art centre of Germany as Paris is the art centre of France. As the Louvre is the pride of the French people, so the Dresden gallery is the pride of the Germans, and if France can boast that she possesses the greatest portrait painted by Leonardo, Saxony can retort that she possesses the greatest picture of Raphael, Leonardo's great successor and rival. Poor

Italy which produced both of them, has neither—but then Italy has enough of others, and to spare. It is worth a trip to Europe, under normal travelling conditions, just to see the Sistine Madonna, the greatest representation of the highest type of mother-love that was ever put upon canvas or that ever shaped itself in the mind of an artist. Most of you have doubtless seen reproductions of the picture—the mother with her infant in her arms and the little winged cherubs at the bottom of the painting. The face does not fascinate one like the mysterious woman of Leonardo; she seems absolutely incapable of attempting to fascinate or bewitch or in any way wield the terrible power that lies back of the calm brow and the magic smile of Mona Lisa. There is only one thing written in the picture, but that thing, St. Paul says is "the greatest thing in the world," for it is love, love for the bright-eyed child she presses to her bosom, love pure, unselfish, divine. If Mona Lisa speaks of power and conquest and the empire of the siren; Mary of Dresden speaks of love, and unselfish devotion, and the empire of the mother.

III. *The Two Types of Womanhood in Contrast.*

These two pictures compromise what may be styled a universal biography of womanhood. The two types of women which have striven for mastery since the foundation of the world are here embodied in the ultimate creations of two of the greatest of world artists. Every girl who is born into this human life of ours sooner or later chooses between them, and forms as her ideal a woman modelled after the one or the other. All the women whose names have come down to us in history range themselves invisibly under one or the other of these two generic types. Under Mona Lisa we may group Helen of Troy, Cleopatra, the serpent of the Nile, Mary, Queen of Scots, Marguerite of Valois, and all of the coquettes and sirens whose eyes have lured men to destruction, who have shattered the peace of individuals and of nations and who have helped to make the world worse because they have lived in it. On the other sides are ranged, Florence Nightingale, the angel of mercy on fields of battle, our own Frances Willard, Elizabeth Barrett Browning, Victoria, the peace-loving Queen of England, and all of the unknown mothers and sisters who have brought sunshine into countless homes and who have helped to make the world better because they have lived in it. To-day the contest is still going on—the unceasing battle between the requirements of "society" and the requirements of home, between the desire to wield the power of the coquette and to become the humble centre of the hearthstone—the never ending conflict between Mary of Scotland and Mary of Dresden.

IV. *The Mannish Woman.*

There is, it should be noted as a passing corollary, another type of woman of which we occasionally hear a good deal in the columns of the press and through the caricatures in the comic newspapers—the so-called "mannish" type, the woman who affects masculine attire, masculine language, and masculine tastes and who does her best, in every possible way, to repudiate her own sex. We have not included her, or him, in this catalogue because, by her own choice, she has placed herself outside the class which we have been considering. The woman who is not satisfied with her birthright as a woman—that is, as the latest, fairest, and most refined of all the creations of God, hardly deserves any further consideration. The attempt to discard that birthright, to paraphrase a well known passage in Hamlet, simply discloses "a pitiful ambition in the poor fool that makes it."

V. *The Siren Type.*

But the first type of woman we have mentioned—the worshipper of Lady Lisa—demands more careful consideration. We find her in every rank and station of society, nay she exists in barbarous lands and in countries where Leonardo's name was never heard and where Leonardo's art was never practised. She lives, it is true, in the royal palace, and her brow of alabaster is bound with glittering circlets of diamonds and pearls, but she lives likewise in the humble cottage and her brow is no less fair because it lacks the diamonds of her sister. There is one altar upon which she sacrifices ruthlessly everything else, and that is the altar of Power. Power to rule men by her smiles and her frowns; power to make women envy her because of her beauty and charm; power to make those who rule the world bow before her, that she may rule them. To such a woman, home has few attractions, and the home which she builds is, in fact, never home at all. Her children are strangers to her, and her husband an article of furniture, differing only from other articles in the fact that he, or it, is alive and has the faculty of voluntary motion. She must live in a style equal to or surpassing her neighbours and her husband must pay for it. If he has the money, it is all right; if he hasn't it, he must get it. Upon the altar which she has built she will sacrifice everything—home, comfort, friendship, religion, and her example penetrates downward through every station of society. The woman with an income of a million wants to live like the woman with a million and a half; the woman with a thousand, like the woman with fifteen hundred, while in the ranks of those with other incomes there is the constant desire to outshine or equal those who have more.

The consequences of this worship of the Lisa ideal are found in the disordered social conditions which America and other countries present to-day. Marriages are becoming less binding, divorces more numerous, while the homes, if the spirit of the real home will pardon my using the name, which this false ideal has rendered unhappy and miserable would be hard to number or estimate. One can understand the temptation which power has for men and women alike, but it is doubtful if any use or abuse of it has wrought the harm and the unhappiness that this worship has brought. And what is the reward? Bitterness and humiliation and disappointment, in the end. The society queen does not rule for a lifetime; the coquette loses her empire as quickly as it is won, and in the bitterness of an old age of blasted hopes and painful recriminations she closes her days. Cleopatra puts the asp to her bosom and dies a suicide; Mary, Queen of Scots, is beheaded in the castle of Fotheringay—the ideal of domination, the society ruler, the coquette, is a false ideal, and behind the smile of Mona Lisa are hidden fountains of tears.

VI. *The Mother Type.*

When we turn to the other picture, the ideal of Mary, how different is the story. In the hurry and bustle of the twentieth century, men are as ready to pay the same homage to true womanhood that they have been ready to pay in the past. Let no one imagine that there is a section of society in existence to-day where the home type, the Mary type, is not longed-for and cherished. The words "For behold from henceforth all nations shall call me blessed" have become a living truth, not only because of the Christ who was born of her, but also because of the sublime type of womanhood for which she stands—a type so sublime that she has become an object of worship for over a hundred millions of people to-day. We need not worship the maiden of Nazareth in order to recognise in her the highest type of earthly womanhood. In her humble life as a village girl, she was taught to be true to the religion of her fathers, to be pure in heart and life, and to be right-minded and sincere in all she did or said. At her quiet village home, the murder of the great and beautiful queen Mariamne was talked about while she was a little girl, and Cleopatra, the mistress of the world, had died probably only a year or two before she was born. How different was her life, the life of the peasant girl of Nazareth, to be from theirs! It is noticeable that there is not very much said about Mary in the gospels nor is there much recorded that she said. The sublime poem of the Magnificat, which formed the substance of our text, contains almost her whole history. And yet there is quite enough said to reveal the nature of the woman deemed worthy to become the mother of the Christ. Her whole life was wrapped up in the life of her child, just as many a mother's life has been since her day, his glory was hers and she needed no other glory of her own. Mariamne, in her proud beauty, might humble the awful Herod before her, and Cleopatra might shine as the ruler of the world and receive the flattery and the homage of princes and nobles, but her empire was of a higher order and her attendants of a nobler kind. Mary suffered much, as the Marys of this world often have to suffer, but she bore her lot with sublime patience and resignation and she has not lost her reward. At the foot of the cross her heart was broken but on the resurrection morn that wound was healed and once more her lips chanted the Magnificat of her girlhood days.

When we are asked to name the dominant feature of her character, but one answer is possible—love. Lady Lisa and her attendants thirst for power and for the gratification of selfish ambition, but Mary is content to sink all thoughts of self in her child and to ask for no power save that wielded by the loving sceptre of a mother. And of all the unselfish agencies in the world is there any quite so unselfish as a true mother? Always, the nearest approach to the divine love has been the love of a consecrated mother.

Next to love, in the character of Mary, came devotion. "My soul doth magnify the Lord, and my spirit hath rejoiced in God, my Saviour." She believed with all her heart in God. She never questioned his existence, his goodness, or his power. He was very real to her. In the morning when she awoke, her prayers went up to him, and at night she fell asleep with his name upon her lips. Well might angels watch her slumber and fill her soul with dreams of Paradise.

After love and devotion in her character, came humility. "He hath regarded the low estate of his handmaiden." How different is this spirit from the pride of Cleopatra which made all of her attendants fear even to tell her the truth, and which exacted homage from high and low alike. The great lessons of Christ's life—The Pharisee and the Publican—the washing the disciples feet and the like, were all lessons of humility but none of his disciples ever learned them like his mother.

Love, devotion, humility—these three form the great trinity which produces the ideal type of womanhood. These three, too, are those characteristics which link humanity closest to the divine. In the life of a true mother there is less of earth and more of heaven.

than there is in any other life that has been or can be lived. When every other influence that makes for good has faded out of his life, the most depraved man cannot forget the mother who loved him in his boyhood days.

What a heritage is a birthright such as this, and what an infinite pity when this birthright is thrown away or sacrificed upon the gilded altars of Society or Fashion or any of the false gods of human invention! When one thinks of these truly terrible sacrifices which are being made every day, he can appreciate something of the pathos wrapped up in those words of Othello which no human tongue has ever adequately uttered: "O, Iago, the pity of it, the pity of it!" Yes, in the light of these supreme tragedies, we may well say—"the pity of it." For, alas, opportunities so tremendous as these: the opportunity of living closer to God, of hearing the motion of angels' wings in the prattle of little children, and of becoming the very incarnation of heaven on earth in the sacred circle of the home, carry with them, likewise, tremendous responsibilities. If it be true that woman can rise higher than man, it is also true that she can sink lower, and the evil deeds of the daughters of earth have written sad pages in the history of the world and in the lives of men. I have often thought that the destinies of humanity are placed much more largely in the hands of women than in those of men. In a very true sense men are not what their fathers but what their mothers make them. There is a passage in one of Coventry

Patmore's poems which every woman would do well
to ponder:

> "Ah, wasteful woman, she who may
> On her own self set her own price,
> Knowing he can not choose but pay—
> How has she cheapened Paradise!
> How given for naught her priceless gift,
> How spoiled the bread and spilled the wine,
> Which spent with due respective thrift,
> Had made brutes men, and men, divine."

VII. *Religion and Womanhood.*

I come back, in my final word, to the song of Mary
—"My soul doth magnify the Lord." There is a Per-
sian proverb which says that a woman without religion is like a flower without perfume. It is supremely
appropriate that "Mother's Day" should be celebrated
in church. It is religion which sanctifies the home and
which makes motherhood the sacred sacrament which
it has become in all Christian lands. May our celebration to-day be filled with that spirit of love, devotion
and humility which was so supremely characteristic
of the ideal mother of the Bible, as well as of her Son
who has become our Saviour and the Saviour of the
world!

IX

(*A Sermon for Decoration Day*)

TEXT: *John* 12:24. "Verily, verily, I say unto you, Except a corn of wheat fall into the ground and die, it abideth alone: but if it die, it bringeth forth much fruit."

LIFE through death is God's law for the universe. The flowers which bloom in all their luxuriance upon the bosom of mother earth; the trees which lift their giant forms toward the heavens; the grass upon a thousand hills; the lily, the violet and the rose: these all live because something has died.

> "Life evermore is fed by death,
> In earth, in sea and sky;
> And that a rose may breathe its breath,
> Something must die."

I. *Life through Death in the Material World.*

There is no birth without death. It may be that the death is only a partial one, but if not complete, it is at least the beginning of the end. That was not altogether a fable, which was embodied in the old story of the Phœnix, the miraculous bird of Arabia. We are told that this wonderful creature lived for five hundred years, and when the time came for the bird to die, it

[100]

built itself a nest in the summit of some gigantic palm tree. With all the strength at its command, it heaped together frankincense and myrrh and sweet scented gums of every kind, and then upon this funeral pyre of its own creation, it breathed its last. And now forthwith, from the dead body of the Phœnix, the infant bird is born and with its gorgeous plumage of gold and green it flies forth in the glory or the sunlight to begin its new career.

The story, I say, is not all a fable. Every day it finds its counter-part in actual life. A mother dies that her babe may live. A father toils unweariedly day after day, night after night, giving a little portion of his life with every setting of the sun, that his child may possess fortune, or education, or success. Will you point to any of the great works of this world, which have not come into being at the cost of life? There is not a marble palace in the universe which is not likewise a tomb. Its massive walls are cemented with blood, and the hollow voices of the dying and the dead are heard above the gayest music of the dance and the carnival, within its halls. The pyramids of Egypt have survived the ravages of time for fifty centuries. For five thousand years the birth song of the springtide, and the hectic glow of autumn's withered leaves have faded beneath their feet. For five thousand years, the sons of men have struggled and bled and died in the sands by their side. For five thousand years, the wedding march and the funeral dirge have alike ascended to the heavens, and they have been silent witnesses. They have stood the test of the

Past, and the Future seems all their own. But beneath the sombre base of the pyramids lie the crushed and mangled bodies of a hundred thousand slaves, who died that they might be built. Beneath the cruel lash of the task-master, they sank down upon the burning sand and died. Tears and blood and agony and death, these things, have purchased earth's longest span of immortality for those massive heaps of stone we call the pyramids.

What is true of past history, is just as true to-day. The New York subway is a sepulchre, no less than a means of transit, and blood has entered into the mortar which lines its walls. Our gigantic railroad systems, which have become the great arteries of commerce and which bear to us the products of every distant land; which have placed New York within sixteen hours of Chicago, and which have enabled us to girdle the world in thirty days, have all been purchased, not so much with dollars, as with lives, and with the tears of the widows and orphans which they have made. In the shriek of every locomotive whistle, if you listen, you can hear the shriek of a dying man, and the fireman who heaps the coal into the furnace of the engine may, by, a slight stretch of the imagination, be said to be building the funeral pyre for some unfortunate being, not unlikely himself. None of us has much faith in ghosts, but if there are ghosts anywhere in the world, they ought to be walking across the ties of a railroad. Our railroads are great and beneficent institutions, but they have cost much in human life, and we are not yet through paying the debt.

II. *Life through Death in the Social World.*

Turning from the mere lifeless creations of brick and stone and iron, to the unseen fabric of national and social life, we find the same story. Our great nation of over a hundred millions of freemen did not spring into existence to the tune of a wedding march, or to the swaying melody of the dance. Its music was of a more serious character. Our fathers died that we might live. Upon Bunker Hill and Long Island and at Saratoga, they poured out their blood like water that we might be free. The bitter privations of Valley Forge, the tracks of blood left in the snow as they marched bare-footed over many a frozen field, are well-nigh forgotten to-day, but it was these things which purchased our independence. Without the sacrifice of life, the generalship of Washington and the statesmanship of Jefferson would have amounted to nothing. Freedom and life were hung in the balance before the eyes of our fathers, and they chose to sacrifice life that they might have freedom.

When you look upon the flag of your country, do you know what it ought to stand for in your mind? I will tell you a little of what it ought to mean. The red stripes signify the blood of your forefathers shed upon the field of battle in crimson streams that you might be free; the white bars stand for the pale cheeks of the widows and maidens, whose husbands and brothers died that you might be free; the blue field with its galaxy of stars, represents the pale blue vault of the heavens into which many a dying soldier looked

[103]

with feverish eyes as the shades of night hovered over the battle field. These all died that America might be free. Who will say that their death has not borne abundant fruit?

"Except a corn of wheat fall into the earth and die, it abideth by itself alone, but if it die, it bringeth forth much fruit." Upon this day, when we commemorate the sacrificial death of the brave men who gave their all for their country, let us think for a moment of the older heroes who died in order that the nation itself might be born.

III. *Life through Death in the Political World.*

Passing on to still another field, let us observe that no great political or national achievement, no great civil victory, has ever been won except at the cost of life. Slavery became a thing of the past in America, but the best blood of the South, and the best blood of the North, were shed that the black man might be free. Some of you who sit before me have wandered over the historic field of Antietam in my own native Maryland. The green grass grows in luxuriance to-day around the old Dunkard church which seems so peaceful and still as you walk around it. There are little blue flowers growing in the grass all about you. Sit down upon the door steps of the old church and look out over the green fields before you and tell me what you see. "Nothing," you say, "except the grass fields and the landscape dotted with homes, and the rugged heights of the South Mountain looming up before you in the distance." Close your eyes before you, and then tell me what you see. If you know the story of the place where you are sitting, there will be another picture before your eyes. Instead of the green grass, you will see acre upon acre of tall swaying corn fields. May will have become September. Around you, stretching far to the south and far to the north, are massed legions of brave men clad in grey. The boom of a hundred cannon sounds in your ears. You look out over the corn field again, and as far as your eye can see you watch a solid phalanx of blue plunging into the tasselled sea of corn, and swallowed up save for the gleam of bayonets which sparkle like diamonds in the sunlight. On they come, company after company, regiment after regiment, brigade after brigade: the bravest of the sons of the North, led by fighting Joe Hooker himself. And then the guns flash in the air, and like the rattle of a thousand hail storms, the roar of musketry is heard. You watch men wearing the blue, and men wearing the grey, throw up their hands, and fall dead and dying to the ground. Then the grey ranks plunge into the blue in one mad, wild struggle to the death. Crash, crash, crash, sound the muskets; cries of soldiers in the agony of death; curses, groans, the clatter of the corn stalks as men bear them to the ground and writhe upon them in pain and in wretchedness; over all, the parching rays of the sun—these things, and a thousand impossible to describe make up the story of the struggle of the day. By and by, night falls, and the stars look down as though in pity upon the dying and the dead who lie in heaps upon the field of battle.

We are a great people, and we are justly proud of our greatness, but we should never forget that back of it are the tears of widows and orphans, the blood and the life of the fathers of our native land. The corn of wheat which produced American freedom was sown on the blood stained fields of Saratoga and Long Island. The full blown flower of the American union was planted as a seed corn in the blood-enriched soil of Cold Harbor, and Bloody Lane, and Gettysburg. The magnificent fruitage of world-wide democracy and peace, which was the goal of our recent world war, will grow from the sacrificial blood shed in the forest of Argonne and upon the blood-stained soil of northern France. Everywhere, alike, the story is one of life through death.

IV. *Life through Death in the Spiritual World.*

These illustrations from the physical, social, and political spheres, but prepare the way for the higher embodiment of the truth in the spiritual and religious world. No religion can exist without martyrs; indeed it has been well said that the blood of the martyrs is the seed of the church. With possibly one exception, tradition records that every one of the twelve apostles sealed his devotion to the faith with his blood. Four of them, it is said, were crucified. Peter, at Rome, with his head downward. Andrew, on the cross which has since worn his name, in Greece; Simon, in Britain, and Bartholomew, by the far-off shores of the Caspian Sea. Thomas was stoned to death; Jude, shot to death with arrows; Mark, dragged lifeless through the streets of Alexandria; Matthew, put to death with the sword in Ethiopia. The book of Acts records the martyrdom of James the Great in the early period of the church's history. John, the one exception to the early list of martyrs, was cast into a cauldron of boiling oil, but, by miraculous intervention his life was spared.

Most striking of all in this respect is the example furnished by the founder of the church, Jesus the Christ, himself. Clad in his tremulous robes of humanity, he shrank from the awful torture of death upon the cross. In the garden, he prayed that this cup might pass from him, as bitter drops of agony fell from his brow. And yet, he realised then, as before, that without the sacrifice of his life his work must prove a failure. In his own case, no less than in others, the corn of wheat had to fall into the ground and die in order that it might bring forth much fruit. And the corn of wheat planted upon Calvary two thousand years ago has borne its abundant harvest in the world-wide progress of his teachings. But before the crown of stars could be placed upon his brow, he was compelled to wear the crown of thorns, and before angels could bear him into the heavens upon the mount of Ascension, he had to be raised aloft by the brutal soldiery upon the cruel tree of the cross. Calvary must precede the resurrection; Gethsemane, the throne above all others in the heaven of heavens.

Since the death of Christ, his church has marched forward by similar sacrifices. The martyrdom of John Hus, who was burned alive a century before Luther, was the starting point of the Protestant Reformation. The fires, which Bloody Mary kindled in England to consume the Protestants, were but the fore-fruits which proclaimed the advent of religious freedom. The intolerant Puritanism of Protestant New England paved the way for the most liberal interpretation of Christianity known in America.

When Ridley and Latimer were led to the stake to be burned for their faith upon that memorable October morning of 1555, the dying words of the older man were prophetic. "Play the man, Master Ridley," he said, as the flames rose around him, "and by God's grace we shall light such a candle to-day as shall never be put out." That candle was the candle of English Protestantism which gave to the world Protestant America, and which largely made possible the advent of our modern civilisation.

V. *Practical Application of the Principle.*

This principle, so true in a greater way, is of deepest significance in our own daily duties and lives. The men who succeed in any work are the men who give themselves completely to that work. We often say that this or the other man is "killing himself" to accomplish some great project. We had better say, that if he is going to accomplish it, he will have to give his life for it. The man who does not shrink from putting his all into a cause runs a good chance of making his cause succeed.

But, after all, the final lesson which I bring to you upon this Memorial day is the greatest lesson, for it deals with the immeasurable future rather than the fleeting life of to-day. The words of the text are of supreme importance as teaching, beyond any question, the true nature of the resurrection from death. Nothing about this human life of ours is ever capable of being fully explained. The wisest man in the universe is like a three-year-old child when we ask him to interpret any of the deeper facts of life. The man who tells us that he understands everything in the world is either a madman or a fool, and the man who says that he understands anything fully and completely, so that there is no mystery left about it, is in exactly the same condition. In the school life of the child there is a stage when it must accept things without understanding them. By and by it understands. So it is with this tangled human existence of ours. Now we are only in the germ state; the corn of wheat has not yet fallen into the ground; by and by we shall put aside the old husk, the new life will spring forth, and then we shall understand. Now we see through a glass darkly, but then face to face. What the new life will be we dare not prophesy any more than the old shrivelled grain of wheat might be supposed to foresee the green blade which springs from it.

These our comrades, brothers, friends, who gave

their all for their native land are not dead. Nay, rather they have found the more abundant life which springs from the spirit of sacrifice, of unhesitating devotion, and of complete surrender to a glorious ideal!

X.

The Supreme Loyalty = to the cause of X

THE SUPREME VIRTUE

(*A Sermon for Flag Day*)

TEXT: *Job* 13:15. (Though he slay me, yet will I trust in him.)

THERE are few good things in the world which do not have their bad sides. There is scarcely a virtue which does not easily degenerate into a vice, or a moral action which may not under other circumstances become immoral. How easy it is for our very best qualities to become the parents of our worst we all know, or if we do not know, at least our friends know. The good man is so well aware of his goodness that we catch ourselves half-wishing that he were not quite so good as he is; the beautiful woman learns to know her own beauty and as a result of that consciousness becomes less beautiful every day; the truthful person is sometimes over-officious about telling all he knows when there isn't any need for it to become public property, while the tactful and kindly person lacks courage to tell the truth when it really ought to be told.

The constant tendency of evil to be present with good is a fruitful source of danger where one might least expect it. There is, for example, nothing more noble than the ideal of the scientist, the constant search for,

[111]

and worship of Truth; the absolute hatred of error of every kind; the ceaseless mid-night vigil for the sake of making humanity wiser and happier: all these, are worthy of the highest admiration. And yet there is a canker which sometimes grows out of this exclusive devotion to science which turns its beauty into ashes and its brightness into shade.

I. *Loyalty, the Supreme Virtue.*

I have referred to the ultra-scientific emphasis upon the present occasion because I believe it to be one of the most prevalent dangers of our modern age. I believe this because it tends to destroy the virtue which this day is especially designed to celebrate—the grand old virtue of loyalty; loyalty to our country, loyalty to our friends, loyalty to our principles, loyalty to our God. The text embodies the most beautiful expression of loyalty recorded in the literature of the world. For ages it has been regarded as the final word in devotion. We need the lesson which it conveys to-day perhaps to an even greater degree than we have needed it in the past.

Before we discuss loyalty, however, let us see just how it is that the scientific training sometimes tends to destroy it. Perhaps the matter can be illustrated best from a simple case of friendship. You have a very dear friend, we will say; you do not know all the secrets of his heart, you do not know all the actions he has committed, nor, if you are a true friend, do you want to know them; you want something that you can take on faith. Perhaps some one accuses your friend falsely to you and you reply at once, with indignation, "The charge is false!" "How do you know?" says the calumniator, "you were not there!" "No," you reply, "but he is my friend; I know him, I believe in him, and you cannot make me believe that he did such a thing!" Now all of this is very unscientific, for science would have said "suspend your judgment until the testimony is all in; then weigh the evidence and decide accordingly." But it is just the peculiar beauty and value of friendship that it would spurn the introduction of evidence; once you go to weighing your appreciation of those you love, just as sugar and coffee are weighed out, then it is time for you to write an obituary of your friendship and you can't write it too soon. The friendship which has to have proof before it will grant confidence; which says, "Let me have a spyglass that I may peer into the innermost recesses of your heart in order to see whether you are a rascal or not": this sort of friendship may be safe in a business way but it is a misnomer to use the word "friend" in connection with it. It is the feeling which a banker ordinarily has toward his patrons, whom he gauges, very properly for his business, according to their wealth or ability to pay. But this business, scientific feeling isn't friendship; it has no element of loyalty or trust about it, and these are needed before one can have a friend.

II. *Loyalty in the Animal Creation.*

Loyalty is one of the virtues which is so deeply interwoven with the whole fabric of existence that we find striking examples of it even among the lower animals. It is, in fact, the most shining of all the good qualities which have so justly endeared many of our animal companions to humanity. The history of the dog family, the most intelligent of all the animal creation next to man, is replete with illustrations of loyalty to master or friend. You remember, for instance, the little pet of the ill-fated Mary, Queen of Scots, who when her mistress was led out to execution, clung to her and fought with all of its tiny power to remain with her even after her head had been severed from her body. I think that next to the consolation which the ill-starred queen doubtless received from her religion, in that gloomy hour, must have been the satisfaction which was afforded her by the devotion of this poor little animal.

There is another well-authenticated record of a dog who when his master, who was a hunter, accidentally shot himself, remained in the woods guarding the spot, although he had neither food nor water for three days. At the last, he had to be shot before he could be taken away. Charles Darwin, who was probably the most thorough scientist that ever lived, displays more emotion in narrating an instance of similar loyalty in the dog than I know of him doing anywhere else. He tells in one of his books of a physician who owned a dog and, moved by that supra-scientific spirit which is the parent of vivisection, he placed the little creature upon the operating table. After enduring torture for hours, the poor animal, just before it died, finding an opportunity, turned its head and extending its tongue licked the hand of its cruel master. And Darwin, cold-blooded scientist as he was, in commenting on the incident says that it was a picture to haunt a man's memory to his dying day. It is questionable whether there is any case in the annals of human devotion which more completely and perfectly illustrates the meaning of the text: "Though he slay me, yet will I trust in him."

III. *Loyalty among Men.*

What is true of the lower animals is also true as you advance farther in the scale. Savages, who hardly know any other virtue, know enough to be true to their chief or true to their clan. The savage Britons clung to Queen Boadicea to the last even after suffering repeated defeats at the hands of the iron legions of Rome. I do not know of more brilliant fidelity anywhere in the annals of history than that which has been displayed by the followers of Mohammed, and it is chiefly this trait which has made Mohammedanism such a power in the world, crude and barbaric as it is in many other respects. Rudyard Kipling, in his famous ballad entitled "Fuzzy Wuzzy" bears tribute to the significance of Mohammedan loyalty:

"So 'ere's to you, Fuzzy Wuzzy, at your 'ome in the Soudan,
  You're a pore benighted 'eathen, but a first class fighten'
    man.
 And 'ere's to you, Fuzzy Wuzzy, with your 'ayrick 'ead of
    'air—
 You big, black boundin' beggar—for you broke a British
    square."

What was it about "Fuzzy Wuzzy" that made him a first class fighting man and enabled him to break a British square. Not a thing in the world but his determined loyalty to the cause for which he was fighting. The presence of this one virtue transformed the black, unkempt, savage, benighted heathen, as Kipling styles him, into a genuine hero, even in the eyes of his opponents in the British army.

As a matter of fact, however, whether a civilised or uncivilised loyalty is the one transcendently brilliant diamond which the dark setting of war has always shown off with the greatest brilliancy, to say a soldier is unswervingly loyal is to pay him the highest compliment in the military vocabulary, and to say he is disloyal is to say the worst thing that you can say of him in a military way. All the great captains of the world were surrounded by a soldiery loyal to the core. The great French general Turenne, who won so many victories, was familiarly styled "Father Turenne" in his camp and his soldiers were incessantly watching over his welfare. In the frightful battle of Lützen, where Gustavus Adolphus, the lion of Sweden, lost his life, when the king fell from his horse, wounded to death, the soldiers threw themselves in heaps over his body, each one determined to die with his master.

Perhaps no man ever inspired more of the sentiment of loyalty among his followers than Napoleon Buonaparte, as selfish a man as I am compelled to believe him in the main. His new conscripts fought with the determined loyalty of old soldiers. Marshal Ney broke his oath to the Bourbons because he could not find it in his heart to be disloyal to his old master. When Napoleon was banished to St. Helena, men fought for the privilege of going into a lonely exile with him.

But not only warriors are recorded as arousing the sentiment of loyalty among their followers. Almost all the leaders of men in civil life have had a similar experience. Pitt and Fox and Sheridan had friends who swore by them and our own Henry Clay was notable among other distinguished leaders of the American populace for the loyalty of his personal following. Every great leader in fact arouses the sentiment of loyalty. The proof of his greatness may be found in this fact rather than in any other.

IV. *Loyalty to Country.*

Flag day is an occasion upon which we are especially called to emphasise the virtue of loyalty to our own nation. This loyalty should, of course, be thoughtful and of such type as to cause our nation and our flag to be honoured and respected throughout the earth. The best way to do this is to see to it that as a nation we embody the ideals of the Founder of our religion to the end that our example may inspire others to do the same thing.

George Lansbury, in his exceedingly stimulating little volume, entitled "These Things Shall Be," calls attention to the fact that no great nation has yet become so thoroughly Christianised as to be able to become a real missionary to other nations. I can conceive of no higher loyalty to America than to resolve to do all in our power to make her just such a nation. The highest type of loyalty is the loyalty which insists upon only the noblest and best career possible for those to whom we are loyal. We must be jealous of the good name of our country, so jealous that we dare not allow her to besmirch that good name by injustice, or oppression, or unfairness, or anything else which our individual conscience cannot approve. There is a petty loyalty which does not think of higher things; which says "my country, right or wrong," instead of saying, as it should, "my country, to be followed when right, and to be set right when wrong."

V. *The Final Loyalty.*

The ultimate and final loyalty of any human being must be to his ultimate and final ideal which means, of course, his God. Sometimes, men have made the state their final ideal and have thus converted patriotism into religion. Certain German teachers before the world war held to this philosophy. It is a dangerous theory because it makes central something which, while it deserves a high place, does not deserve the highest position in a man's thought or life. It is the teaching of the Scriptures throughout that we must love the Lord our God with all our heart, with all our soul, with all our mind, and with all our strength. The Old Covenant laid down as its first requirement that no other God should enter into rivalry with Jehovah for the affections of his people. Everywhere the story is the same. Our highest loyalty must be God: Anything else than the highest means that we have no loyalty at all.

There are two propositions that our practical sense teaches us must be true: First, man is by nature a religious being, and second, there is but one religion which calls out the highest and the best that our human nature embodies. These statements are made with only the most courteous reference to all other religions. The greatest danger to-day is not from those who have intellectual difficulties concerning Christianity, but it is rather the danger which arises from the habit of fickleness, from the prevalent under-tow of disloyalty which sweeps away so many thousands of men and women. It is not that we are dissatisfied with our flag, but simply that we have gotten ourselves into that frame of mind which will not permit us to be truly loyal to anything. And so, after a time, we are blown about by every wind under heaven and we are not sure that we owe allegiance to anybody or to anything. We are lost in the true sense and we are lost because of our disloyalty.

There are many people, in this modern age, who seem to think that there is something noble about the sort of independence which is ready to leave an old service at any time and pick up a new one; which goes before its commander with a chip on its shoulder, and which says, "I will leave you when I like, and I will obey you when I please." But for my own part, I must confess that this spirit appears the reverse of admirable. Of all the men in the world there are none so hopelessly useless and disappointing as those upon whom one is never able to lay his fingers. There is no habit so dangerous, either for this world, or for the next, as the habit of fickleness. At all costs, have some sort of principles and stick to them. Be loyal to somebody or to something. One of the most beautiful of the old Greek stories is the legend of Antigone, who, when her brother fell in battle, because the victor had issued a solemn decree that anyone should be buried alive who attempted place the body in a sepulchre and no one would risk the danger, at last went herself and yielded up her own life that her brother's dead body might have the benefit of the last rites of his religion. The story is very old, and has been immortalised by the genius of Sophocles, but it remains fragrant and inspiring even to-day. In Christian literature, there is no more beautiful picture than that which is presented in the action of those women who watched heart-sick by the cross and went early in the morning to the sepulchre. What a contrast between them and the traitor, Judas, who embodies the Biblical type of disloyalty! Even a bad cause is illumined by the loyalty of its followers, while a good cause is glorified thereby. In all the annals of religious history there is no crown for the traitor, and no garlands for his memory. The crown is always to the one who overcomes, who endures to the end, who is faithful and loyal even unto death!

XI

THE UNREAD LESSONS OF LIFE

(*A Commencement Sermon*)

TEXT: *Luke* 10:26. "How Readest Thou?"

THE question propounded in the text is of interest both by reason of association and of its own practical meaning and import. A certain lawyer, skilled in the knowledge of the Prophets and in all the traditions of the Jews, stands up and tempts the Christ with a query as old as history itself: the never-ending problem of the ages, "Master, what shall I do to inherit eternal life?" In reply, the Master, with one of those flashes of delicate irony, which exhibit his power most fully, propounds a counter-question: "What is written in the law?" he says, "How readest thou?"

Now, this man was a lawyer. Not only had he read the law, but as his apt power of quotation indicates, he had it practically at his tongue's end. He was doubtless familiar with the text and every shade of formal interpretation. From his lofty standpoint of technical scholarship, he no doubt looked down upon the Nazarene carpenter who presumed to instruct one so learned as himself. But in a few moments, through the power of a simple illustration, the immortal parable of the Good Samaritan, vanquished and crestfallen he retires from the fray. He is forced to admit, tacitly, if not otherwise, that he had never read, in the true sense, the Law and the Prophets which parrot-like, he could repeat by rote.

The race of lawyers of the kind mentioned in the text is not yet extinct. In the universal library of the Creator, there are many books provided for the instruction and profit of the sons of men. With these volumes, all of us are more or less familiar. Many of their pages have been committed to memory; some of us, perhaps, know even the foot-notes to the text. Yet, after all, our lives, which are the only real tests of the true extent of our knowledge, indicate, too often, I fear, that we have not read them in the true sense of the word.

I. *The Book of Nature.*

There is first the great book of Nature: The lesson of the sunshine and the clouds; of the passing of the rose, and of the fading of the violet; of the withered leaves of autumn and the budding foliage of spring. What do we read in the rapid succession of birth and death in the plant and animal creation all about us? Perhaps, few of us like Shakespeare, can find sermons in stones or books in the running brooks, and fewer still, like Shelley, the divine whisperings of prophecy in the sighing of the western wind, but all of us, from the least to the greatest, should find some lesson of importance in the book of the flowers and the stars. Consider, if you will, the course of a single day; how it begins in gladness and life, in the morning; how it goes on to the meridian of heat and life, and, how in the haze of the afternoon, it slowly fades away until the shades of evening fall. Is there not in its passing a suggestion of the transitory nature of life and the coldness of the tomb? It is as though God has given us the very days themselves, with their various phases so strikingly parallel to the course of life as a whole, to remind us, with every setting of the sun that soon we too shall have run our race and soon the grave shall have received us into its bosom. But the days come, and the days go, and the lesson of the day remains unheeded. "How readest thou?" my careless friend, in the volume of the hours.

Again, there is a chapter in the book of Nature devoted to the flowers. "Flowers," said Henry Ward Beecher, "are the sweetest things God ever made and forgot to put a soul into." What a lesson there is in a simple blade of grass; a lesson which Moses has put into the solemn words of the ninetieth psalm: "In the morning they are like grass which groweth up. In the morning it flourisheth, and groweth up; in the evening it is cut down and withereth." So too, there is something singularly pathetic in the life and death of a rose. Delicately, it puts forth its leaves under the influence of heat and moisture; slowly, and little by little, the exquisite bud is born, and then each day new graces come with the dawning of the suns, until, at last, beneath the kisses of the dew and the smiles of the stars, the full-orbed rose bursts into life. Life,

alas, soon to be followed by death, for the seeds of
dissolution were sown in the moment of its perfect
bloom. How the rose seems to say to you, if you
will listen to her words; "as is my life, so shall be
yours; however beautiful, or wise, or brilliant you may
be." "How readest thou?" my youthful friend, in
God's book of the flowers.

Again, there is another chapter in the book of Nature
devoted to the animal creation, as distinguished from
the plant and the vegetable. Here, the most important
section is that which deals with man. There is no
study quite so interesting as the study of personality.
There is more in a human face, than there is in a hundred manuscripts. There is more in the throbbing
pulsing heart-life of the humblest man or woman that
ever lived than there is in the roar of the ocean, or the
majesty of the mountains or the hills. Men with their
passions and their sins; men with their blunders and
their mistakes; men rising to the heights of heaven on
the wings of poetry and song, and men sinking to the
depths of hell in the dens of vice and shame. Over
the graves of our friends, are there no inscriptions of
warning for us? Does the funeral procession passing
"with dirges due in sad array," arouse in us no thought
of a similar procession in which we shall figure, not as
the mourner, but, perchance as the person mourned?
"How readest thou?" O careless sceptic, in the book
of the lives of men, well may it be for you, if with
the soothsayer of Anthony and Cleopatra you can say:
"In nature's infinite book of secrecy, a little I can read."

II. *The Book of Conscience.*

Time bids us close the volume of Nature and take up another book from the universal library of God. This time it will be the book of Conscience; the Law of the Inner Life. What means the sting of remorse; the feeling of self-condemnation and shame? Is there not something strange about this inner monitor which, with no visible appearance whatever, has forced strong men to suicide, and has driven its possessor to the gallows by a voluntary confession of guilt? One of the most striking criminal cases in the early history of the United States was that of the murder of Captain White of New England. An old man, without an enemy in the world, one night he was murdered in his bed for the purpose of robbery. No eye, save the un-sleeping eye of Jehovah, saw the murderer as by the light of the moon he lifted his victim's arm across his breast and plunged the fatal dagger into his heart. The deed was accomplished with such precaution that no suspicion fell upon the murderer. Unknown and unsuspected, he walked among his companions and was safe from the scrutiny of man. But a Power greater than that of detectives or magistrates pursued him. In his waking hours, he saw a knife, blood-red to the hilt, ever before his eyes, and whenever he fell asleep it was always to dream of the moonlight; not the moon, as it had appeared in the days before his hands had become the hands of a murderer, peaceful and serene, but rather blood-red, like the sun half-hidden behind a cloud. At last, the struggle becomes unendurable

[125]

and then the suicide of the unhappy wretch proves his confession of guilt. Conscience has a thousand several tongues, and all of them inform against the guilty soul of the criminal. They speak of obligation to some Higher Power; they speak of judgment, of sin, of condemnation. If no other book were open to our gaze, the book of Conscience alone would furnish sufficient evidence to make us think seriously of the warning it conveys. "How readest thou?" my brother, careless about the future, in the book of thine own conscience, and the moral nature of man.

III. *The Book of History.*

A third book in the universal library of God is the great book of History—men's doings and lives since the story of the ages began. There is no study more profitable than history if it be studied as it should be: there is no study so profitless as history, if it be studied as it usually is. The mere knowledge of names and dates is, for the most part, an encumbrance to the mind and a weariness to the soul. Nevertheless, to him who reads aright, history furnishes some splendid lessons. Dionysius of Caria, the old Greek philosopher, said truthfully that history is only philosophy teaching by examples. One of the most striking lessons of past experience is what may be styled the significance of the unnoticed in human experience. It is the little things, the unnoticed things, the unread lessons which have always determined destiny.

We talk, sometimes, of the insignificance of speech

and the trifling value of a syllable, and yet the tragedies of the past and of the present, nay, the history of the future that is to be; the sublime heights of a heaven and the awful depths of a hell, have more than once been held fast-bound within the charmed circle of mortal accents. Nations have trembled at the power of an unspoken word. There was an hour in the life of Rome, the mistress of the world, when her last army lay crushed upon the field of battle; when her sword was shivered for the third time by the Punic legions; when out of eighty thousand in the morning scarcely seventy soldiers rode back with Varro in the shades of evening; when the courage of tribune and the daring of dictator could not hope to defend the walls of a city stripped of all its warriors; when the Fates seemed to have cut the thread of national existence and the sun of glory and of victory to have set amid the carnage of Cannæ's fatal field. Then, in that hour, fraught with peril and dangers and death, there came an unexpected salvation only through the order that was never given, through the word that was left unspoken, and Rome, Rome with all her significance for future ages, Rome was saved because Hannibal shook his head!

There is nothing little in the annals of life or of nature. Some trifling word, a careless blow, a simple smile, a feather blown before the wind, have formed before, may form again, links in the massive chain of Fate which stretches unto all eternity. Be it the sarcasm of a Maintenon, making untold orphans in the sunny vales of France; be it the sword-thrust of a Martel, saving civilisation and Christianity from the hordes of Moslem invaders; be it the angelic smile of a Genevieve, averting from Paris the dreadful consequences of a barbarian's wrath; in all, through all, there rises a veil of perfumed incense to heaven, and on the broad expanse of the firmament we can trace the glorification of the almighty power of little things.

IV. *The Book of Revelation.*

Once more, and for the last time this morning, we turn to the universal library of God and pluck forth a volume. This one is entitled the book of Revelation or of Revealed Truth. Its contents are more direct and plain than are those of any of the others we have seen, so far as the most important issues of destiny are concerned. It has survived the rage of persecution and the hostile sneers of criticism. It contains the story of a life like no other life and a history which is unique among the chronicles of man. The King of Heaven throws aside his glory and descends to earth to live the life of a peasant and to die the death of a slave upon the cross. He suffers indignities of every kind, he submits to cruel treatment and scourging: He, the King of Glory and one with the Eternal God Himself. Was all this done being needless or a matter of no particular value? Do we not, when we lessen the danger from sin, lessen the value of the cross? It is easy to talk in smooth-flowing phrases about the universal salvation of mankind, regardless of effort or character, but the bitter suffering in the garden and the cry of agony upon Calvary, speak of something more serious, and a danger not imaginary but real. We may not like to think of the rapids; we may refuse to believe that they exist; but when those who love us give their lives to warn us of the danger, if we perish, with whom lies the condemnation?

The book of Revealed Truth contains three lessons of especial significance for the consideration of every human being. These three lessons may be stated in the following language: First, God is Love; second, Sin is Death; and third, there is a Judgment.

The first of these lessons is not revealed in any of the books which have just been considered. Stamped on every page of the book of Nature, we can read these words: "God is Power"; indelibly written upon the tablets of the human heart and of the human conscience, there is likewise engraved the sentence: "God is Justice"; but only in the book of Revealed Truth do we find in clear and unmistakable terms the sublime message that God is Love. It is only through the Incarnation that the goodness of God can be proved. God is love because Jesus Christ is God, and Jesus was the perfect embodiment of love in the realm of human experience.

The book of Revealed Truth emphasises in a very special way the reality of sin and the danger of its consequences. Simple and plain as its language is upon this all-important theme, too often it is not read. Dishonesty among those in high position, scandals in every department of life; corruption and vice on the part of those who profess their faith in the church: these things would be impossible if men read the book of Revelation. Our modern age does not like to read passages like these: "The wages of sin is death," and "The soul that sinneth it shall die"; hence men make a Bible to suit themselves, and cut out what does not fit. But the Book stands the test of the scissors as it has already stood the test of the flames; it lives, and some day, by its teaching its critics shall be judged. A man does not remove the sun by putting out his own eyes. He no longer sees, it is true; but the sun is still there. So a man may refuse to believe God's message in whole or in part, but its truthfulness is not affected by his refusal to accept it. If he sins, and remains in his sins, he shall die; whether he believes there is such a thing as death or not. The Pharisaical life, no less than the sneer of the sceptic, or the lukewarm indifference of the average man of the world find no comfort in the pages of revelation.

Last of all, the book of Revealed Truth contains a lesson of Judgment. There is a picture drawn by the Son of God himself of that scene when amid the thunders of heaven and the collapse of a universe of stars, the Son of man shall come with all the holy angels and with great power and glory. Doubtless, this language is to be interpreted in harmony with the oriental imagery which characterises so much of the Scriptures, and yet it certainly conveys a sublime truth. If there is a moral order in the world, that order demands that absolute justice shall be done, sometime, somewhere, and we know that absolute justice is not done in the round of our material existence. Immanuel Kant, the most profound of modern

philosophers, has based his proof of immortality
this fact. Here, at any rate, he is in harmony
Scriptural teaching. There is no fact more clearly
explicitly stated in the pages of the New Testam
than the fact of a final judgment.

But the time for closing the books has come. To
you who stand upon the threshold of active participa-
tion in the busy affairs of life the lesson of the morning
must be clear and obvious. Whether you succeed or
fail in the supreme business of existence will depend
upon how you read the lessons of both past and present
experience. If you go down to defeat and failure in
the end, it will not be because there have been no
warnings given you; it will be because you have refused to read the plainest and clearest messages of
your Maker. May your record be such that at the close
of the day you may be able to incarnate those words
of the author of Thanatopsis:

"So live, that when thy summons comes
  To join the innumerable caravan that moves to that mys-
    terious realm
  Where each shall take his place within the silent halls of
    death
  Thou go not like the quarry slave at night
  Scourged to his dungeon. But sustained and soothed
  By an unfaltering trust, approach thy grave
  Like one who wraps the drapery of his couch about him
  And lies down to pleasant dreams."

XII

THE LIFE WORTH WHILE

(*A Commencement Address*)

THE history of success, and the history of failure is the history of the same thing viewed from two different standpoints. Whether the landscape before you is tinged with blue, or covered with green; whether the horizon appears clear or darkened with clouds, may depend entirely upon the colour of the glasses which are placed before your eyes. If you wear green glasses, everything will look green, if you wear blue glasses, everything will look blue; and sometimes I have thought that there are some people who make a specialty of wearing blue glasses all of their lives.

In much the same way, if you want to know what a young man is going to make out of life, all you need to know is the standpoint from which he habitually looks at the world, and himself as a member of it. Is it simply a playground in his eyes; or is it a workshop? Is it a place to make money; or to have a good time? Is it an orderly universe; or is it all a strange, mixed up, inexplicable chaos, of which, he himself, is the most inexplicable feature?

I. *The Proper Viewpoint.*

The attitude one takes toward the questions just mentioned will largely determine his life, but the master influence of all will be his attitude toward this question: "Is my daily life an end in itself, or is it a means to a higher end?" Or, as the theologians are fond of putting it, am I living for a time, or am I living for eternity?"

It would seem rather unnecessary, upon an occasion such as this, to mention in any questioning sort of way the age-old theme of personal immortality. Outside of juvenile debating societies and metaphysical class rooms, we are satisfied, for the most part, to let what has been said on the subject, and there has certainly been enough said, suffice without addition or comment. We no longer regard it as a question in dispute. It is a part of our religion, it is presupposed in our laws, it enters as a matter of fact, into our entire social fabric; and yet, when one looks at the daily life of the average man, it is an open question as to whether he really believes it, or is only trying to delude himself, as well as others, into the idea that he does.

This may seem like strong language, but, I ask you frankly, is it not justified by the facts? Do you think, for instance, that if a man were absolutely and thoroughly convinced that the character which he is building every hour and every day, just as surely as a mason builds a house, brick by brick; that this character is something which will last forever,—do you suppose, I say, if he believed this, that he would have told the falsehood he did tell for the slight gain he hoped would result from it, only an hour before? If a young man were absolutely sure that the impression which he knows, the books which he habitually reads are producing upon his mind is something he will have to carry about him forever, do you suppose that he would read the questionable literature which he does? What is true of the careless falsehood and the vulgar book, is just as true of the obscene jest and the immoral life. There is always a good deal of intellectual scepticism in the world but it is never a tithe of the practical scepticism which exists. There are people, for example, who repeat the Apostles' Creed with unction and fervour, and who, so far as their intellects are concerned, are no doubt sincere when they say that they believe in the resurrection of the body and the life everlasting, who, nevertheless, in their actual lives are neither better nor worse than if they were disciples of Paine or Voltaire. They are not theoretical but they are practical sceptics. To them might be applied the language of one of the great masters of English prose upon another occasion: "what you are speaks so loud I cannot hear what you say."

This practical scepticism is nowhere more apparent or more disastrous than when it influences the choice of an ideal for life. The tendency of the modern age appears to be to discount the practical value of belief in a future life. A great many of our modern educators for example, leave the question of personal immortality entirely in abeyance. They build for time exclusively; they lay no foundation for eternity. But, if it be true, that the soul is immortal, then assuredly the supreme question which every educator ought to have in view is this: "How can I mould the plastic mind which is placed in my hand so that it will develop into something that is really worthy of immortality?" It is a light matter, and a comparatively easy one, to educate with reference to a particular business, or a particular profession, so far as this world goes, but to play the architect for a structure that is to last forever: this is an entirely different thing. And yet every parent, and every teacher is doing this consciously or unconsciously day after day. The first and most important step toward realising the life worth while is therefore to resolve that everything said and everything done shall be said or done with the ideal of personal immortality thoroughly before the mind.

II. *The Ethical Ideal.*

It is a great thing to get the right viewpoint, and to stick to it, but this is only the beginning of the problem. Granted, in a general way, that our rule shall be always to have in mind the ideal of making something out of our lives that shall be worthy of immortality, the next question is, along what specific lines shall we proceed in order to make our ideal real in our own lives?

First in time, and first in importance I unhesitatingly affirm is the training of the Will; the formation of character. The teacher, for example, who teaches for eternity, rather than for time, will have no patience with the education which is purely intellectual, or which is even primarily so. The education upon which he will insist will be ethical through and through, and there will be no uncertain ring about its ethics either. The great trouble with most of our modern systems of training is that they do not treat the ethical question as though it were as important as the intellectual. When their graduates go out into the world they are smart enough but they are not upright enough. They have sufficient brains to secure a position, in a city bank, but they do not have sufficient character to keep them from stealing several thousands of dollars of its funds as happened in a case I recall a few years ago.

Now there is not much hope for an ethical bankrupt in time, but there is even less for him in eternity. His intellectual ability has nothing whatever to do with it. There is no name in the long line of English jurisprudence which is so cordially detested and abhorred as the name of George Jeffreys. It is not because he was a dullard or a weakling, for he possessed an intellectual acumen which would have been a credit to any lawyer of his day. But he was a moral bankrupt on the side of humanity. He scented blood like a tiger; his courtroom was the den of a wild beast, and when he entered it to take his seat, half intoxicated, his cheeks on fire, his eyes staring like a madman, even the boldest pleader was helpless before him. He ordered the court hall when he held sessions at Dorchester, after the Monmouth rebellion, to be hung with scarlet, and condemned the widow of a member of Parliament, Alice Lisle, by name, to be burned to death simply because she had given food and drink to two weary soldiers of the Rebel army. At a sitting of a few days at another place he sentenced two hundred and ninety-two people to be hanged. He died at the age of forty-one in the Tower, the state prison of England, where he had been sent at his own request that he might not be torn in pieces by the people. "At his death," says Macaulay, "he was hated by all classes with a hatred which is without a parallel in English history." Assuredly, there must have been something wrong with the ideal of life of a man who could die at the age of forty-one, leaving such a record behind him, after having been Chief Justice of the King's Bench at thirty-five, and Lord Chancellor of England at thirty-seven.

Jeffreys was a moral bankrupt on the side of humanity. There was a brilliant American of the same profession who was a bankrupt on the side of fidelity. When Aaron Burr graduated at Princeton College nearly a century and a half ago, he made a record for scholarship which has never since been equalled in the history of the college. No more brilliant genius was ever born on American soil. If Aaron Burr had possessed the strength of character to have matched his intellect, there is scarcely a doubt but that his name would stand to-day as high as any name in American history. But Burr was a moral bankrupt. He was faithful to but one thing throughout his life and that thing was his own ambition. He violated at will the most sacred ties of nature and society; he gambled on the virtue of his innocent acquaintances; and he never made a promise in all his life except with the idea of breaking it, if he believed it would pay him to break it. He died at last at an advanced age, a ruined and broken man, leaving such a record behind him that it was with difficulty that his ashes were allowed to rest in the burying place of his father. In the old Princeton cemetery there lies a plain marble slab, now half chipped away by the relic hunters. On this slab there is the following simple inscription:

AARON BURR

A Colonel In The Army Of The Revolution
And Vice President Of The United States.

The tradition used to be current during my school days at Princeton that the body which sleeps beneath that tombstone was placed there after night, for the simple reason that it would not have been permitted to have been placed there in the daylight.

Jeffreys and Burr were lawyers; with them, I wish now to link the name of one of the greatest philosophers of the ages, the founder of modern science: Francis Bacon. Bacon was not inhuman, like Jeffreys, nor faithless like Burr, but he was so weak on the question of money that he tarnished one of the most brilliant careers in the annals of history with a stain which his most indulgent biographers cannot wipe away. It is pitiful to think that a man with such transcendent genius could condescend to accept the miserable bribes which were offered him, but we have his own confession that he did so. Hence it comes that for Bacon, the scientist, and for Bacon, the philosopher, all ages will have respect and reverence, but for Francis Bacon, the man, there will only be more or less of pity mingled with more or less of disgust.

In comparison with the genius of the three men I have just mentioned, the name of William Wilberforce sinks into insignificance; and yet, after his death, a grateful people erected a monument to his memory upon which was inscribed the following epitaph, an epitaph which is worth remembering: "The eloquence of his silver tongue has ceased, but the eloquence of his noble deeds will live forever."

There are a good many people who laugh at Puritanical ideas of morality, and yet these same people never sleep half so well, when they are in a strange country as they do when they are lodged in the house of a Puritan. It is because of the integrity of the men whom they pretend to despise that they are enabled to go to rest at night without the apprehension of being robbed of all they possess. As Woodrow Wilson used to put it in his classroom: "some men possess integrity of character and all men get the benefit of what some men are."

The experiment of non-ethical education has been tried among nations and it has been tried among individuals, and it has failed often enough for people to think seriously of discontinuing it. The great difficulty with the ancient Greek civilisation was its defective ethics. So far as philosophy and art are concerned, the culture of Greece will probably never be surpassed, but its religious system deified thieves, drunkards, and murderers, and placed an adulterer on the throne of Olympus. Certain modern nations appear to be following in the same pathway, and if this should prove true, they are destined to end at the same goal. The polite and cultured Parisian shrugs his shoulders in wonder at the Puritanism of his neighbours across the Channel, but when he consults the statistics of the population and growth of his native land, he finds that it is retrograding at a rapid rate, and that, from the present outlook, it is only a question of time, when it will be swept out of existence in the great struggle for survival among the nations.

It makes no difference what theory of morals we accept; whether we regard morality as the voice of God in the soul of man, or whether we regard it as the product of innumerable experiences inherited and preserved through an indefinite period of time; the fact remains that the man or woman who discounts the ethical element in his life is gambling his or her future, both for time and for eternity upon the most frightful risk conceivable by man. If it be true that the moral consciousness is of divine origin, then our action in defying it amounts to defying the Almighty, in the very Holy of Holies of his Sanctuary. If, on the contrary, it be true that morality is only the product of innumerable experiences inherited and preserved through an indefinite period of past time, then to defy this product means simply to stake one experience against uncounted millions of them with the hope that the lottery of fortune will turn out the one prize among the millions of blanks.

The master mind of the universe, at least in a literary

way, has drawn three wonderful pictures of men, all of them of consummate genius, who tried to defy the moral laws of the world and to come off unscathed. All of them failed. Richard III, after the most brilliant exhibition of energy and intellectual vigour, falls at last on the field of Bosworth and his crown passes into the hands of his deadliest enemies. Edmund, in the play of King Lear, after plotting against his brother and all of his relatives, and after succeeding in the most unexampled manner, sinks at last, never to rise again. The conclusion of his experience is found in the line uttered when he is at the point of death: "the wheel has come full circle; I am here;" yes, here in the dust, with my enemy's sword above my head—here at last—the wheel has come full circle! Iago, in the play of Othello, the fiend in human form; the personification of what the most brilliant intellect is apt to become when unchecked by moral restraint; the most skilfully drawn character of the most skilfully constructed play of the dramatist: he too, at the last, gets his reward and sees his finely woven net of villainy torn into atoms by the moral power of the universe. Nobody, so far as I know, has ever accused Shakespeare of writing his plays to prove any great moral lesson. Everywhere and by everybody he has always been considered as the great copyist of Nature; the man who never struck a false note after her, or varied a shade in the tints which he painted after her colouring. It is no light matter, therefore, that he should have drawn three of his greatest characters as men who exerted almost Titanic powers of intellect to overcome the moral laws of the world, and in every case made a miserable failure.

"Character," says Emerson, "is Nature in the highest form; it is of no use to ape it, or to contend with it." Solomon is still regarded as the sage of all the ages; the cherished intellectual idol of three great religions, and yet with all his wisdom, by his own confession, his life ended miserably and a failure simply because he did not think it worth while to obey the moral law. "If only Robert Burns had possessed a moral balance," says one of his biographers, "what miseries might he not have averted for himself, what might he not have become for the ages!" I have seen grand old white-haired Theodore Cuyler stand in the chapel at Princeton University and say, after enumerating the advantages of the school in an intellectual way; "gentlemen, the grandest product of this grand old university is a noble Christian character." There is a solidity, a reserve power, as Emerson styles it, about the man of integrity which is consciously, or unconsciously acknowledged by all who come in contact with it. Those who do not possess it, pay it the same sort of reverence which the demons were wont to pay to the Son of God. In times of great trial and perplexity they feel safer in the presence of a man who possesses this type of character than they do anywhere else.

Out in the Yosemite valley there is a magnificent mountain peak named El Capitan, rising thousands of feet into the air, with its base sweeping back into the Sierra Nevadas. There are earthquake shocks felt in that section, and when the guide is asked what the people do when they fear the earthquake, he replies; "they go back to El Capitan and they stand upon its base, for they say that when El Capitan falls, then falls the world!" Character is the El Capitan of the little world of the individual, and when it falls, then falls his world.

III. *The Intellectual Ideal.*

But man is not all Will any more than he is all Intellect, and because character is of first and primary importance is no reason why of itself it should be all-sufficient and complete. A fool is probably of more use in the world than a knave, but that is the best that can be said of him. No man respects a dullard, even though he be of princely birth. "I have tried Prince George drunk and I have tried him sober," said King James of England, "and drunk or sober, there is nothing in him. He is not worth as much as a trooper in my guards." Sins of or against the will are mostly sins of commission; sins of or against the intellect are mostly sins of omission. It is a sin of omission of the most grievous type not to develop to our utmost power, the intellectual strength which God has given us. "This god-like reason," in the words of Hamlet was not bestowed upon us "to fust in us unused." You doubtless remember, in the same play that wonderful catalogue of the powers of man in which we are told: "What a piece of work is a man! How noble in reason! how infinite in faculties! in form, and moving, how express and admirable! in action,

[143]

how like an angel! in apprehension, how like a god!
the beauty of the world! the paragon of animals!" All
this man is, or may become but in order to become it
he must develop the intellectual powers which God
has given him. There is something sublime, I had almost said divine, about the manner in which the mind
of man can enter into the secrets of all the ages, of
how it can commune with sages and philosophers innumerable; and thus, with all of his relative insignificance, man is enabled to carry the very key to the
universe within his brain. How admirably the sage
of Concord has expressed this idea in the opening lines
of his Essay on History:

> There is no great and no small
> To the Soul that maketh all:
> And where it cometh all things **are;**
> And it cometh everywhere.
>
> I am owner of the sphere,
> Of the seven stars and the solar year,
> Of Cæsar's hand, and Plato's brain,
> Of Lord Christ's heart, and Shakespeare's strain.

Yes, you who sit before me, may think the same
thoughts that Plato thought; may thrill with the same
emotion which Shakespeare felt when he wrote his
marvellous dramas. Moreover, this intellectual power
is something permanent. We cannot carry our stocks
and bonds, our houses and land, with us into the other
world; into the eternity which lies ahead of us, but
the mental capacity which we develop is something
which will go with us wherever we go: it is a fund of
which we can never be made bankrupt. There are just
three words in the epitaph of the historian Green, who

wrote the best popular history of England ever produced, but they are three words worth remembering: "He died learning." Whatever may be our lot in the next world, I do not believe that it will be to stand still. We shall need all of the capital we can take along from this existence, and next to the character which we develop will come the intellectual capacity and grasp which we make our own.

IV. *The Esthetic Ideal.*

A man, however, is not entirely Will, nor is he entirely Will plus Intellect; he is also a creature of Emotions and Feelings; in other words, he is esthetic as well as ethical and intellectual. No worthy ideal of life can afford to neglect this latest, and in a certain sense, most brilliant side of personality. To enumerate what the individual misses who fails to develop the artistic side of his nature would be to enumerate a long and important list of items. Take, for instance, the case of music; what an inspiration it is, even to those who know but little about it; what an intoxication of the spirit; what a heavenly fire! It is said that there will be golden harpstrings in heaven, and we are wont to look upon it as a place where all of the scattered rays of earthly musical talent will be united in one harmonious unison, but what will all this amount to if one has no appreciation of the sound of a harp-string?

Much the same thing is true of the allied fields of

poetry, of painting and of sculpture. Our esthetic enjoyment depends, almost entirely, upon cultivation. Almost every human being has the germ of artistic appreciation within him if he will develop it. If he fails, to give it attention, it will die still-born, and he will become an esthetic bankrupt for time and, so far as we can see, for eternity. Moreover, the artistic faculties must be trained in youth; money cannot repair the damage after the season has passed in which they should have been cultivated. "A man," said Doctor Patton, upon one occasion, "may have the fortune of the money-kings of the universe; he may live one-fourth of the year in town, and one-fourth in the country, and another fourth at the seashore, and he may spend the remainder of his time in Europe, but there are some things which his money cannot buy. One of them is a delicate appreciation of artistic beauty. If he has not nourished the germ which God gave to him in his youth, in his old age he will find it withered and dead, and when he enters eternity, he will enter it bankrupt upon the side of esthetic appreciation.

The life worth while will be achieved when we view things, as Spinoza said, "under the form of eternity," instead of under "the form of time," and also when in the light of this higher viewpoint we learn to develop every side of our nature in a free, harmonious, and symmetrical way. This is the highest goal which any human being can place before himself as the essential business of life. It is, indeed, the "summum bonum" of human endeavour.

V. *Practical Conclusions.*

There is nothing, I suppose, which causes the careful thinker who really believes in the immortality of the soul, so much wonder as the manner in which men and women habitually neglect the opportunities which this world presents for self-development, along worthy lines. To make a living; to become famous or wealthy; even to outshine our neighbors in society: all these are objects of much seeking, but to make something out of ourselves that is worth lasting forever,—this is apparently the last thing most of us think about. The majority of old people see the truth when it is too late for them to do much to repair the mistakes that have been made. The best and greatest of the old men that I have known have made this confession, often with infinite pathos and regret. I do not suppose that any man ever had less to regret in this direction than Theodore Cuyler of New York, to whom I referred a few moments ago. And yet, I remember hearing Doctor Cuyler say, after he had reached the age of eighty years, when he was asked if he were afraid of any spectres in heaven: "yes, I am afraid of the spectres of lost opportunities!"

"I do not wonder," says Ruskin, in the famous lines which Drummond has seized and made immortal, "at what men suffer, but I wonder often at what they lose." Life looks long to a young man and it doesn't seem to him to make such difference what he does day after day, and hour after hour, but by and by he gets a vision of the whole thing in a clearer light, and then he sees that every day and every hour were of infinite importance and that every momentary thought helped to make him the man that he finds himself to be. "You shall give an account of every idle word in the day of judgment," said the Greatest of Teachers, and no truer words were ever uttered. Yes, every idle word enters, infinitesimally though it be, into the grand total which makes you, and you must account for yourself at the last. The law of development is inexorable. The personality of a man is not built up in a day. People often think that they can do things which will leave no impression upon their souls. There can be no greater fallacy than such a conception. When you enter the next world, you must enter it as yourself; you cannot enter it as anyone else, to think of doing so, would be only to think of your own annihilation. Therefore, the all-important question; the question that, if I had the power, I would burn as with some corrosive acid into the mind and heart of every person in this room, is this: "what kind of a self have I? Is it worth lasting forever? if it is not, why isn't it?" What sort of a heaven would you feel at home in? It is said that a dog's heaven is a door-mat before the fire, and some men have not much higher ideal before their minds. Life, it has been said, is like a fast express train, running between two points, which we designate as Birth and Death. As the train sweeps along, some of us look out the windows; some of us read; some of us do nothing; some of us even pick our neighbours' pockets: but by and by, there comes a slowing-up of the brakes; the gong sounds; the trip is over, and the train whirls off with other passengers. Whatever we have done, has been done; whatever we have left undone, must always remain so.

I have only one word more. The life worth while cannot be achieved without the firmest confidence in an all-wise, an all-powerful and an all-good Captain of our souls. We need not quarrel over points in theology, but unless we believe in a God, from whom we can hide nothing, and to whom we must all render account, all our character building will be weak and all of our symmetrical development will be slow.

There is a tomb in St. Paul's Cathedral in London which has no body within it because the body has never been found. One day, two little boys entered the cathedral, evidently from the lower strata of London society. The one led the other, who, it was easy to see, was blind. They passed by the statues of kings, and sages, and poets, and every now and then the one boy would stop and say to the other "is this the one?" and his little comrade would step up and feel the monument with his hands and say, "no," until at last they reached the monument under which there was no body, and then they both stopped and the little boy went over it carefully with his fingers, seeing with the eyes of the blind, and then the two went out in silence. The monument was that of General Charles George Gordon, Chinese Gordon, they used to call him, who was killed at Khartoum, in the Soudan, and whose body was never recovered. Gordon took for his motto, early in life, the words which every young man or woman in this graduating class would do well to enshrine in memory: "never tell anybody to do anything that you are afraid to do yourself." It is the inscription upon the tomb in St. Paul's, however, to which I wish to call special attention because it tells the story, not only of the secret of the success of Gordon's life, but of every other life that has been truly worth while. These are the words of the epitaph: "He gave his strength to the weak; he gave his sympathy to the suffering; he gave his substance to the poor, for he had given his heart to his God."

Without God no life truly worth while can be lived; with him such a life may easily become a glorious reality. It is only in the full consciousness of such an achievement that we can look out toward the future and say with Alfred Tennyson:

> Sunset and evening star,
> And one clear call for me!
> And may there be no moaning of the bar,
> When I put out to sea.
>
> But such a tide as moving seems asleep,
> Too full for sound and foam,
> When that which drew from out the boundless deep
> Turns again home.
>
> Twilight and evening bell,
> And after that, the dark!
> And may there be no sadness of farewell,
> When I embark;
>
> For tho' from out our bourne of Time and Place
> The flood may bear me far;
> I hope to see my Pilot face to face
> When I have crost the Bar.

XIII

THE EVOLUTION OF NATIONAL IDEALS

(*Independence Day Sermon*)

TEXT: *Psalms* 72:7. "In his days shall the righteous flourish; and abundance of peace so long as the moon endureth."

THE story of the beginning of governments is a very interesting one. In the earlier history of the world men lived in separate families with the father of the family as the sole law-giver. The code of laws was, of course, oral and dependent upon the will of the patriarch. As the family developed into the clan, and the clan into the tribe, and the tribe into the kingdom or the state, little by little the foundations of written law were laid. At first, these laws were very crude, because the people for whom they were made were no less crude, and law is always intended for the people, never the people for the law. Law is, in fact, nothing more than crystallised public sentiment, and never can be anything more. The conflict over laws arises because public sentiment is always in a state of ferment, and in every case the old teaching holds over by virtue of its position until the new can clearly establish its place. A people's laws are not, and cannot be any better than the general sentiment of the nation. I remember hearing Woodrow Wilson say in his Jurisprudence class at Princeton that the Czar was the best governor for Russia until Russia itself put him away. Of course, he said, that there were doubtless at that time millions of people in Russia who had gotten even then beyond the Czar, but there were many more millions who had not reached that stage in development. Since the time this remark was made, Russia has overthrown the Czar, public sentiment having reached a stage where the monarchist rule no longer represented the voice of the people.

I. *The Progress of Evolution—Earlier Stages.*

Law is the servant of the people at large just as every individual considered by himself is the servant of the law. For this reason, national ideals must be evolved and become recognised before they can be crystallised into laws. In the early history of the world, progress was slow. In the three fundamental spheres of personal rights, family rights, and property rights, only the simplest rules prevailed. In the sphere of personal rights, safety of life and limb was the goal of the earlier, as it has been of the later laws of nations. The methods, however, by which it was guaranteed have changed almost infinitely for the better. In the family sphere, while things are still far from perfection, much progress has been made. In the palmiest days of the Roman Code, a man might put his wife to death without any hindrance from the law for the most trivial offences; for example, if she purloined the key to his wine cellar, or if she tasted wine without his consent, and for other derelictions of similar character. In the terms of the Roman law woman was denominated, not a person, but a thing. To-day, she has at last achieved equal rights and privileges under the law.

With regard to property rights, laws have multiplied and higher ideals prevail. For one thing, human slavery, which in early history was universal, has disappeared almost entirely from the face of the globe. Another improvement has been in the enactment of laws prohibiting cruelty to domestic animals; still another, the destruction of property rights, when they become a nuisance to the community at large. In Shakespeare's day, only four centuries ago, every citizen, if he cared to do it, could keep a garbage heap before his front door and no man could say him nay. This too, even though the neighbour's family took the fever and died as a result of unsanitary conditions. In these earlier days the common sense of the community took no note of the most ordinary axioms of general welfare.

II. *Further Stages of Evolution.*

The progress of national and social ideals is admirably shown by going through some of the castles and prisons of the older time. In London, you will find rusted models of the rack which a few centuries ago was ordinarily and pretty universally used to pull people's bodies apart until they told anything to get rid of the pain. In European prisons you will find worse things in existence than even the rack. Nowadays, they torture a witness by cross examination but, with a few occasional exceptions upon the part of ignorant and brutal public officials, in no other way. Two or three centuries ago, the rack and other instruments of torture were in common use all over Europe.

Another thing which has gone along with the torture is the custom of arbitrary imprisonment. Before the days of Habeas Corpus a man could be arrested at any time, kept in jail any length of time, and given no chance to establish his innocence. In the days of the French kings, Louis XIV and XV, only a little over a century ago, the king signed blank forms of arrest, and a favourite of the king filled them in. The unhappy wretch whose name went in the blank was arrested some dark night, hustled off without a chance to say good by to his family, and buried alive in the Bastile or some other dungeon of the king. The French Revolution made that sort of thing impossible forever.

Still another evil which is disappearing rapidly, but which has not yet quite disappeared, is the union of Church and State, or the enforcing of religious views by the secular arm. No provision of the United States Constitution has met with the general approval of our people more than its doctrine of the separation of Church and State. It is everywhere recognised that religion is, and of right must be, purely a matter of conscience, and that the arm of the civil law has as little to do with a question of conscience as a gadfly has to do with the higher mathematics.

III. *Our Responsibility for Future Progress.*

It is not so much the history of the past, however, which should concern us to-day, as it is the problems of the future. It is true that we should be grateful for what has been accomplished, but our duty does not end in effervescent gratitude. Upon our shoulders lies the burden of to-day and the responsibility for to-morrow. Much remains to be done, and in the few minutes which are allotted for this sermon I can hope to do no more than to mention briefly a few of the more important ideals which are in the most immediate need of realisation.

One of the first which should be mentioned is the ideal of humaneness, if I may put it in that way. This refers to a number of excrescences which still burden the body politic and help to encourage pessimism among decent people. One side is the child labour question which has been so largely discussed in recent social reform literature, and to which one of America's foremost poets has largely devoted his life. We have done a great deal to elevate the living conditions of the ordinary labouring man and woman. Much remains still to be done before every human being is given a fair chance to make the most of his life.

Another consideration which demands attention is the problem of prison reform, and the treatment of criminality in general. One phase of this question relates to the mediæval character of our legal executions in many presumedly civilised commonwealths. The matter of capital punishment itself may be left out of discussion, but the barbarity of method is beyond apology. The time will come, and before very long too, when the gallows will be exhibited along with the rack and the guillotine and the garrote as specimens of days of forgotten barbarism. A little over a hundred years ago, capital punishment was inflicted in England for over a hundred offences. That is, the law said it should be so inflicted. If a man stole sheep, he was to be hanged; if he broke into a house to pilfer, he was to be hanged; if he stole over five pounds (twenty-five dollars in our money), he was to be hanged; if he resisted arrest, he was to be hanged; if he defaced Westminster bridge, he was to be hanged. Of course, the consequence of all this was that eventually no jury could be found to return a man guilty of these crimes. If a man stole ten pounds, or twenty pounds, or fifty pounds, the jury would find that the amount did not exceed four pounds and nineteen shillings in order to save his neck. And so, by and by the Draconian laws slid off the statute books. To-day in certain sections of America popular sentiment has gotten so strong against capital punishment that it is a common thing at a murder trial for scores of presumptive jurors to be disqualified because they do not believe in the infliction of the death penalty for any cause. In my own home county, in one of the eastern states, it is extremely difficult to secure a conviction of murder in the first degree. In the case of the only capital sentence which was imposed in that county for years the condemned man was not hanged because of the pressure brought to bear upon the governor for a commutation of the sentence from the very section where the crime had taken place. Perhaps as a people we have not yet evolved to the point where we are willing to rid the land of the barbarity of legal executions, but it seems to me that we ought to be rapidly approaching it. Beyond any question the recent war has turned the clock backward in this particular respect, as well as in countless others. Nevertheless, we ought to recognise the fact that the disappearance of cruelty in any form is, and always has been, the distinguishing mark of the upward progress of civilisation.

In this connection, attention should be called to the increase of lawlessness throughout our country as a whole. The mob spirit has shown itself with renewed emphasis since the recrudescence of animal passions in the world war. The barbarity of many of these exhibitions of mob violence cannot be duplicated outside of the records of the Inquisition or of Middle Age criminal procedure on the continent. It is time for Christian people throughout our land to awaken to the necessity of maintaining law by peaceful procedure in order that we may wipe out the terrible stain which the mob spirit is fast placing upon our history.

IV. *The Most Important Future Ideal.*

Perhaps the most important ideal of all, and the one which is receiving most consideration nowadays is the ideal of world wide peace. It is possible that we are not yet quite civilised enough for universal peace, but it is to be hoped that we are heading rapidly in the direction of it. Just what the practical result of the recent disarmament conference will be we cannot say, but the mere fact that such conferences are being called is an item of no little importance. The infinite folly of war, the stupidity of settling disputes by brute force instead of by the common reason of mankind, will some day become apparent to everybody and then the torpedo boats, and the armored cruisers, and the battleships will go to the museums, and the war budget, which now swallows over ninety per cent of our funds, will be spent building libraries and colleges and parks and public roads and art galleries and in providing comforts for people instead of providing approved methods of killing them. The day when the swords will be beaten into plowshares and the spears into pruning hooks is sure to come, and it may be nearer than most of us think.

V. *The Moralising of National Ideals.*

One of the hopeful signs of the future, in which we are all especially interested at this time is the withdrawal of government protection from immoral agencies. That the nation should become a silent partner in the perpetuation of vice and vicious habits, thereby lending aid to agencies which have for their aim its own destruction, is a form of suicide as peculiar as it is indefensible. Of course, the drawback hitherto has been the toleration or indifference of public sentiment. It is gratifying to say, however, that things are progressing toward a higher level. Lottery schemes have been put under the ban of the law, and gambling, which has been a function of government many times during the past, no longer has the support or approval of the state. It is an exceedingly disgraceful thing, that vice is still harboured in certain sections under the protection of the law, and that, on the ground of expediency, it has found defenders among the ranks of professedly decent people. It is only a question of time when this attitude must, and will change. Of the three chief foes of social progress, gambling, social vice, and the saloon, the first and the last, after making the most strenuous fight for legal tolerance, have at last been put under the ban. The saloon was fought energetically in city precinct after city precinct, in crossroads town after crossroads town, in county after county, state after state, until the national sentiment became crystallised to the point where it was outlawed by the voice of government itself.

VI. *Concluding Corollaries.*

The advocates of this or the other reform sometimes forget the necessity for the slow and gradual, but none the less sure and powerful development of public sentiment, in order that permanent progress may be made. The prophet has such clear perception of future needs that he is apt to become impatient because things move so slowly. But things must move slowly at first, and after all they move more rapidly than many of us imagine. The function of the true reformer is to blaze the way; to keep hammering at the problem; to beat down prejudice; to endure calumnies; to suffer persecution, detraction, and misunderstanding, but at last to win the goal. The public at large is a great unwieldy sort of animal which has to be coaxed at times, and goaded at times into what is necessary for its health; perchance, even for its salvation. But when the unwieldy animal is once fairly set in motion the reform soon comes. This too, is preeminently the mission of the pulpit. It is the chief business of the preacher to develop national ideals as well as to emphasise the individual welfare of his auditors. To keep men's eyes fixed on the true goal of individual and social life; on something higher still to be realised; to fight the agencies which are pulling in the downward direction; assuredly the pulpit can have no greater mission than this. Moreover, this is the special reason for the existence of memorial occasions, like Independence Day, when in the light of past sacrifices, we rededicate ourselves and our nation to the task which lies ahead.

The life of a man and the life of a nation can rise no higher than the goal which is placed before them. Against this goal there is always the constant pressure downward, the desire to stand still, which always means to go backward, so that progress is only achieved by constant effort and struggle. "Look thou not down but up," is the watchword of success in the moral, social, and the national realm. He only is a true citizen who strives, day by day, to develop higher national ideals, and by adding his own mite of effort to the cause of righteousness brings the gates of the Golden City a little closer to our view.

> "Be what thou seemest, live thy creed,
> Hold up to earth the torch divine,
> Be what thou prayest to be made,
> Let the Great Master's steps be thine.

> "Fill up each hour with what will last,
> Buy up the moments as they go,
> The life above, when this is past
> Is the ripe fruit of life below."

XIV

THE MODERN WORSHIP OF MONEY

(*Labor Day Sermon*)

TEXT: *Ex.* 32:8. "They have made them a molten calf, and have worshipped it."

IDOLATRY is not the heritage of a single race or a particular period. It is the crime of the civilised man and of the savage, of the bondman and the freeman, of the inhabitant of the jungle, and of the fashionable patroller of Rotten Row, or of Fifth Avenue. Of course, the names and the appearance of the deities have changed. We no longer worship Ashtoreth with the obscene ceremonies which excited the horror of Isaiah or Jeremiah; we no longer rear huge statues of brass to Moloch and burn our children alive in their hideous arms while the beating of countless drums drowns the cries of the hapless innocents, as they did in the days of Ahab and Manasseh; we no longer construct a literal calf of gold, as did the children of Israel in the desert, but if anybody imagines that the spirit of idolatry, the spirit of Ashtoreth worship, or Moloch worship, or the worship of the Golden Calf is dead, he is very much mistaken. Ashtoreth is worshipped nightly in London and in New York, and all over the civilised world with rites which would have put heathendom to shame; her shrines are erected, not only among the poor and vicious, but in the palaces of the rich and the society leaders of the metropolis. We do not burn our children alive in the arms of a brazen deity nowadays, but if you will ask a reputable surgeon of any of our larger hospitals, he would tell you more children's lives are sacrificed every year to unnecessary and false social requirements than were burned in all the ages, in the literal worship of Moloch.

I. *The Golden Calf in Our Modern Age.*

We laugh at the idea of worshipping an image such as Aaron made for the half civilised Israelites, but the smile has not disappeared from our faces before we get down on our knees and prostrate ourselves before the invisible calf of money that rules pretty nearly everything in civilisation to-day. How careful we are not to insult him; how elastic our opinions become; how reversible, if need be, our political views; how made-to-fit-the-occasion our religious attitudes. It is terribly hard to convince a man that anything is a sin if he is making a lot of money out of it. There is "Sin" written all over the centre of the work he is doing, but his spectacles have a blind spot in the middle so that he cannot read the word; moreover, if anybody else reads it for him, he gets angry and says it isn't there.

There are a great many evils which afflict humanity to-day, but the evil which reaches the farthest and hurts the worst, is the evil which the Apostle Paul said was a root of every kind of crime in his day: the love of money. The love of money perpetuates the reign of intemperance and vice; protects and apologises for bribery and crime; oppresses the poor; is the prime factor in perpetuating militarism and war; produces all forms of civic corruption, and ruins the empire of the home. More than this, it enters the church and poisons its efforts to raise humanity to a higher level. There are ministers, no less than laymen, who worship the Golden Calf rather than the Living God, and whose prayers are too heavily freighted with gold to ever rise above their lips.

Let us notice very briefly how this universal Mammon worship has affected the life of the American people. In the first place, it has created a false ideal for the young. If you go through our greater American colleges to-day, you will find that the chief ambition of the great majority of the boys studying therein is to get rich, and not only to get rich, but to get very rich. There are more pictures of John D. Rockefeller and Andrew Carnegie hanging in the rooms of college students to-day, than there are of Benjamin Franklin or Thomas Jefferson. Their ideal is a money ideal. Moreover, that money ideal is not always linked up with the highest conception of honesty in its attainment. Some one has expressed the motto of the age in this fashion. "Money is the principal thing, therefore get money. Get it honestly if you can, but by all means get it."

Then again the modern worship of money is primarily responsible for bad government and for the dishonest management of great offices of public trust. That was a sad spectacle which was enacted some years ago when a United States Senator over three score and ten years of age, who had served his state and people for over twenty years, was sentenced to imprisonment in his old age because of dishonesty, due to his love of money. The extent to which lobbying and bribery are carried on in both state and national legislation is a matter of open and public scandal. Bribery is a sin as old as Philip, the father of Alexander the Great, who said he could always capture a city after he had introduced therein a mule with a sack of gold on its back. Sir Robert Walpole, of England, was responsible for the maxim: "Every man has his price." Francis Bacon, the founder of modern science, stands pilloried before the ages because he accepted bribes, by his own confession, to the amount of forty thousand pounds. Bribery, therefore, is nothing new, and yet, I have been assured by those who are in a position to know, that if the public generally were aware of the legislation in America that has been passed and kept from passing by lobby influences during the last half century, they would open their eyes in astonishment.

II. *Golden Calf in Business.*

This pernicious state of affairs in national life, finds its apt counterpart in great business and industrial concerns which affect a large number of people and which are frequently controlled by a few. There are those present who will recall the great life insurance scandal of some years ago, which laid the foundation of the political fortunes of Charles E. Hughes. It will be recalled that Mr. Hughes brought out the fact that in some of these companies salaries were ostensibly paid to dead people (just who really got them does not yet appear to be clear); salaries were paid to people for no service rendered whatever; contributions of money collected from policy-holders of all political parties were paid to the campaign fund of one party; outrageous and unwarranted expenditures were made for office furniture and the like. The worst thing about it all was that this money so recklessly squandered came from the hard earned savings of thousands of policy-holders all over the world, who were paying large premiums, often denying themselves the necessities of life that they might save their policies from lapsing and in this way protect their families. This insurance investigation, revealing as it did, the insatiable greed for money on the part of leading business men is to my mind one of the most disgraceful pages in the history of the social life of America. Life insurance is one of the great blessings which have resulted from the progress of science, but its honest management is imperative. The highway robber of ancient times who held up passengers and relieved them of their purses rarely took any money from a poor person, or from one who had but little; nowadays, however, the love of money appears to find its chief scope in the robbery of the poor. It will be recalled that the strongest language used by the Christ during his ministry was applied to those hypocrites who devoured widow's houses and within were full of extortion and excess. It was to this class that he applied the famous anathema of Matthew 24: "Ye serpents, ye generation of vipers, how can ye escape the damnation of hell."

III. *The Golden Calf and the Home.*

A third instance of the injurious effect of the modern worship of money is found in its influence upon the home. I shall not presume to go into detail concerning this phase of the question. It is my own judgment, however, that greed has broken up more homes, shattered more domestic bliss, and caused more dissension in families than any other one factor in the world. This has occurred, for the most part, in two ways; first, by extortion and oppression from without, which includes all unjust exactions of capital in any form, or of the oppression of one man by another; and, second, by the love of money in the heart of those who make up the family themselves, making them perpetually dissatisfied with their lot and station in life, and ever longing for more. The thirst for money is the most relentless passion known to the human soul. It will doom millions of human beings to famine and torture; it will sacrifice virtue, morality and religion; it will plunge nations into the inferno of war; it will wring its dirty coin out of the heart's blood of widows and orphans; it will ally itself with intemperance, vice and crime; in short, there is noth-

ing in the whole category of diabolism which it will
not encompass in order to secure its ends. The evil
influence of this worship of the Golden Calf upon the
homes of America is one of the strongest indictments
which future ages will bring against the inherent
selfishness of modern industrialism.

IV. *The Golden Calf and the Church.*

Worst of all, if there be a worst in the catalogue,
is the influence which the worship of money has had
upon the church. The epistle of James is largely
directed against the difficulties which had already arisen
in the church because of the inordinate love of money
on the part of certain of its members. "Go to, now,
ye rich people, weep and howl for your miseries shall
come upon you. Your riches are corrupted, and your
garments are motheaten. Your gold and silver is
cankered; and the rust of them shall be a witness
against you, and shall eat your flesh as if it were fire."
The Apostle Paul, in his letters to Timothy, repeatedly
referred to the danger of worshipping money instead
of giving wholehearted devotion to the service of the
Lord. "Those who are eager to be rich," he says,
"get tempted and trapped in many senseless and pernicious propensities that drag men down to ruin and
destruction. For love of money is the root of all
mischief; it is by aspiring to be rich that certain individuals have gone astray from the faith and found
themselves pierced with many a pang of remorse."
It is one of the crowning glories of the religion of
Jesus Christ that it overthrows all artificial social

barriers and barriers of caste. Before God, we are all equal; the rich have no higher distinction than the poor, and so it is in every church which is seeking to embody and to proclaim the ideals of Christ. Too often to-day, however, the church, like the world, bows before Mammon; is afraid to speak the truth for fear it will offend the unrighteous power of wealth, and forgets that it is certain to lose the power of God just in proportion as it sells itself to God's greatest enemy.

One of the most striking scandals in the universal Christian world is the lack of harmony and co-operation manifested by the followers of the Christ. In the Intercessory Prayer given just before the arrest and crucifixion of Jesus, he prayed that all of his future disciples should be one in the same sense that he and the Father are one. That prayer has not yet been answered. One of the grandest steps ever taken in the direction of answering it was the organisation of the Young People's Society of Christian Endeavour. Interdenominational in its scope, it would seem that it should have secured the favour of all denominations. But after a while there were various secessions from it, and its influence in the field of unity was largely curtailed and destroyed. The New York *Independent*, in commenting on the situation, remarked editorially that what stood in the way of the universal acceptance of the Christian Endeavour programme was "the interests of publishing societies," and the editor, who at the time this was written was Doctor William Hayes Ward, added further that the ultimate cause was "the love of money, the source of most evils."

Surely, there is no place in the world where the love of money is seen in quite so hideous a form as when it soils the white robes of the church. I can understand, in a measure, how politicians, accustomed to seeing and handling what is worst in social life, can be brought to sell their souls for money; I can understand how a bar-keeper, or a gambler, reared amid vicious surroundings and feeling shut off as by a ban from better society can do the same thing, but how any one professing to handle the oracles of God and to speak in the name of Jesus Christ can do this is beyond my imagination.

V. *The Golden Calf and Labour.*

We ordinarily think of the worship of money as being the exclusive characteristic of the rich man, or of the capitalist. As a matter of fact, however, there are many people with but little money who worship Mammon at heart quite as much as those who have more. The man who wills to be rich is, from the moral point of view, in the same class as the man who actually possesses the wealth which the other man would like to possess. The curse of our modern industrial order is selfishness, the worship of the Golden Calf on the part of both rich and poor. Until we can rid ourselves of this disease of the soul there will be no peace in the body politic. We must cease our idolatry, learn to think in unselfish, instead of in selfish terms, and in this way help to bring in the Kingdom of God.

It should doubtless be added, as a corrective corollary

that because the worship of money is the great sin of our modern age is no reason why we should abandon the use of money itself as a medium of exchange. Money in itself is neither good nor evil. People were covetous before money existed, and if it should ever be abolished, they will doubtless remain covetous. It is the spirit of selfish competition, the animal lust for selfish gain, the jungle attitude toward our neighbours which is responsible for the situation. We must undergo a change of heart, we must come to see that our interest in the good of humanity as a whole must count for more with us than heaping up gold for ourselves. We must, in short, learn to worship Christ instead of worshipping Gold if we are to save ourselves and the world from the perils which surround us.

After all, when we come to think about it, there is much, in fact all that is eternally worth while, that money cannot buy. It cannot buy peace of mind or of conscience, as a great many bad people have found out; it cannot buy artistic appreciation or any of the finer touches of the intellect: these things come only with patient labour and effort. It cannot buy reconciliation with God, or the pardon for sin, for only a broken and contrite heart can purchase these. But though it cannot buy any of these things, yet all of them may be sold for it; and because they are daily being sold and because men are daily going down to ruin on account of this fact, I plead for a different spirit in the hearts of those who listen to these final words. I impeach the Mammon of modern civilisation, in the name of the young men and women in whose hearts it is implanting false ideals of life, ideals which will mean disgrace and ruin at the last for them and their homes; I impeach it in the name of our own fair land whose strength it seeks to sap in the halls of popular government; I impeach it in the name of the homes of America which it has entered too often to blight and to destroy; last of all, before high Heaven, I impeach it in the name of the Church of the Christ himself, the Christ whose last prayer it has sought to render of no avail and whose sacrifice on the Cross it has belittled and scorned!

XV

THE DEATH OF THE GODS

(*An Address for Armistice Day*)

AT the conclusion of Part I of his book entitled "Thus Spake Zarathustra," Friedrich Nietzsche, who claimed to be the Anti-Christ and who must assume no slight responsibility for the horrors of the Great War, gave expression to the following sentiment: "Dead are all the gods; now do we desire the Superman to live."

Not in the way that the half-mad philosopher intended them, and yet in a very true and real way, his words are already approaching realisation. The most significant thing which has been going on in the world during the last six years has not been the slaughter of men, nor the destruction of property—it has been the smashing of ideals. And inasmuch as the only practical definition of the Deity which is conceivable must always be expressed in terms of an ideal, the process may very fairly be entitled—"The Death of the Gods." A man's God is always his highest ideal, and, conversely, his highest ideal is always his God. And now, as never before, the old ideals of the past, in government, in politics, in religion, and in education are going to smash—dynamited by the "Busy Berthas"; shot through by the shrieking shrapnel; buried past resurrection beneath the abysmal mud and squalour of the trenches. Of a truth, the old gods of the past, or at least most of them, are dead.

The slaughter of the gods is nothing new in the history of humanity. In the early days of savagery, every nation had its god. This god was regarded as a sort of extra defence in war and in times of great peril to the tribe or to the nation. About one-half of the cuneiform inscriptions of the ancient Babylonians and Assyrians are devoted to statements like these, which I have copied verbatim from George Rawlinson's translation of the inscription of Tiglath Pileser I, an Assyrian king who ruled about 1150 B.C.:

"In the service of my lord Asshur, my chariots and warriors I assembled. I set out on my march. The exceeding fear of the power of Asshur, my lord, overwhelmed them. . . . At this time, in exalted reverence to Asshur, my lord, . . . there being found no equal to me in war and no second in battle, to the countries of the powerful kings who dwelt upon the upper ocean . . . the lord Asshur having urged me, I went." And so on the record reads interminably.

Now if we substitute the German word "Gott" for Asshur in this record, written over a thousand years before Christ, it sounds for all the world like a modern Prussian war bulletin.

The ultimate test of all these gods was, of course, pragmatic. If the nation had bad luck in war the chances were that it tried a new deity. The principle was something like that of the little boy who announced

[174]

to his mother, one evening, that he was not going to say his prayers any more. When she inquired the reason for this decision, the youthful philosopher replied—"Well, I didn't say them last night and nothing happened, and I am not going to say them to-night and if nothing happens again, after this I am not going to say them at all."

Of course, the idea of the Deity, in the cases to which we have been referring, was fundamentally one of superstition or magic. As men advanced in the scale of civilisation, they gradually substituted moral concepts or ideals for the cruder notions of their earlier years. They pinned their faith upon, and guided their lives by, certain great principles of thought and action. Now when these principles go to the scrap-heap they are inevitably discarded, in the same way that our savage forebears gave up the worship of Asshur or Nisroch, when Asshur or Nisroch no longer "made good" in the fields which they occupied.

I want to talk about four of these principles or ideals in the realm of modern civilisation which I believe the world upheaval is fast sending to the scrap-heap. I shall designate these four gods of the past, for the sake of clearness and brevity, by the following titles: Scientific Materialism, Aristocratic Privilege, Religious Formalism, and Narrow Nationalism. All four have been mighty gods in the cultural circles of the last century and all four, I believe, are dead, past recall, as a result of the recent world war. As thoughtful men and women, it is our business to bury them and to reconstruct our social and educational systems without them. They are dead, anyway, as Lazarus was before his resurrection and, if we mistake not, the signs of putrefaction have already set in. It is time to roll the boulder against the door of the sepulchre and to shut it up forever.

I. *The God of Scientific Materialism.*

The first god to which we have referred—the God of Scientific or Rationalistic Materialism—was the great god in the educational world of the last century. His coat of arms was a chemical retort and a brace of pipkins and the crown of laurel which he offered his devotees was a Ph.D. degree from Berlin or Leipsic. He proclaimed the new rule of scientific investigation as the be-all and end-all of human progress. His followers scoffed at religion, and especially at Christianity, as being only a relic of superstition and as beneath the consideration of the scholarly mind. They boldly prophesied a new era in which science should be the only religion and in which humanity should march to perfection under the banner of Comte or Haeckel. And humanity has marched—to the perfection of gas bombs and machine guns and long distant cannon able to kill unoffending civilians at a range of seventy miles. This god has sent out men from our great universities trained to invent and use every device of intellectual ingenuity to maim and torture and destroy their fellow creatures. This god has let loose the Turks upon the helpless Armenians, and

[176]

has then issued university manifestoes to justify the fiendish deeds of massacre and wholesale extermination which followed. This god has torpedoed little children and women in the supreme agony of woman's existence on the *Lusitania,* has, Paderewski tells us, killed practically all the little ones under seven years of age in Poland, has filled the lungs of thousands of men with chlorine gas on the Western Front and left them to choke to death after days of inexpressible torture and has let loose every demon of cruelty which Satan had hitherto kept under leash in the unseen world of diabolism. Of a truth it is time that this god were dead and buried, before his worship proves the suicide of the human race.

I do not wish to be misunderstood here. I hold no brief against science as science. Science is right and proper in its place. What I am objecting to is the deification of science—the making a god of it. It is the worship of this god which constitutes what the greater part of the world has come to know and loathe as KULTUR. KULTUR is only another name for the God of Scientific Intellectualism and of Materialistic Efficiency over which our modern age has gone wild in a riot of frenzied idolatry.

Henry Churchill King in an address delivered in Washington a few years ago, before the close of the war, said that when the representatives of the warring nations gathered at last around the council table there would be a place at the head of the table reserved for a figure clad in scarlet. This figure, if asked its name, he said, would reply: "I am the Incarnation of Destructive Science." It is time to chain this false God of Kultur, of Destructive Science, and to hurl him down to the bottomless pit where he belongs. It is a case of Michael slaying the dragon or the dragon slaying Michael and our prophecy is that Michael will win. Nay, we shall go farther and say that Michael has won. German KULTUR, the God of Materialistic Science—or of Scientific Intellectualism—is to-day deader than the ghost of the late departed Cæsar.

II. *The God of Aristocratic Privilege.*

The second god in the social and educational realm which humanity will elect to get along without in the days to come, is the God of Aristocratic Privilege. This god has ruled the human race since the dawn of recorded history. He is the incarnation of the caste spirit with all which that term implies. From the very beginning, there have been two classes in the world: the masters and the slaves. We talk about the democracy of ancient Greece or Rome, but the truth is that there was never any real democracy in either nation. Even in cultured Athens, at the height of her civilisation, for every freeman in the population there were from a half-dozen to a dozen slaves. The situation in Rome and in other nations was still worse. The lot of a slave in these older times was wretched almost beyond the power of imagination. The inhuman punishment of crucifixion was devised in the first place as a means by which to terrorise the slaves. If a master thought he detected signs of insubordination on the part of his servants, it was no unusual thing to have one of them crucified in order that his prolonged agonies might serve as an object lesson to his comrades. It was one of the taunts commonly hurled upon the early Christians that the God they worshipped had met the ignominious fate of a slave. After long years, a third class, what the French call the bourgeois or middle class, gradually made its appearance between the two classes of masters and slaves. In time, also, the slave became the proletariat or working man. But throughout all these changes, the God of Aristocratic Privilege has retained his sceptre. Always there has been a privileged class which has thought only of itself and has left the rest of humanity "go hang." Always this ruling or privileged class has taught the doctrine that the weak are to be exploited for the benefit of the strong, and that society is rightly made up of two constituent elements—the one to be trampled upon and the other to do the trampling. Always these selfish aristocrats, whether kings or nobles or priests or militarists or capitalists or whatever other title they may wear, have manifested the most callous indifference for the men and women who grind out their lives that their lords may have an additional thrill of pleasure. Hear George Moore, one of the typical representatives of the group in our own day, who possesses the merit of saying plainly what the others think but do not often say aloud:

"What care I," he says, "that some millions of wretched Israelites died under Pharaoh's lash or Egypt's sun? It was well that they died that I might have the pyramids to look on, or to fill a musing hour with wonderment. What care I that the virtue of some sixteen-year-old maiden was the price paid for Ingre's painting—The Source, that exquisite dream of innocence, to think of till my soul is sick with delight of the painter's holy vision. Nay more, the knowledge that a wrong was done,—that millions of Israelites died in torments, that a girl or a thousand girls, died in the hospital for that one virginal thing, is an added pleasure which I could not afford to spare."

And he goes on further to say:

"That some wretched farmers or miners should refuse to starve that I may not be deprived of my demi-tasse at *Tortoni's*—is monstrous."

Doubtless it seemed monstrous to him and to the other selfish aristocrats whom he represents that "some wretched farmers and miners should refuse to starve" in order that he and his companions might loll in the lap of luxury, but the point is that since this war they are going to refuse. It was in hot indignation against this sort of thing that Robert Burns wrote his famous lines:

> "You see yon birkie ca'd a lord
> Who struts and stares and a' that,
> Though hundreds cower at his word
> He's but a coof for a' that."

And yet when Burns wrote those lines he knew that, in actual fact, they pictured what ought to be rather than what is. He knew that the "birkies" had the bit in the mouths of the hundreds who cowered before them and that they proposed to keep on strutting and

staring and applying the whip and spur. I hold no brief
for the Bolsheviki, but I can read, and any intelligent
man who cares to do it, can read in the language of
that proletariat revolution in Russia the inevitable
handwriting on the wall, unless the God of Caste, the
God of Selfish Class Rule, in short the God of Aristocratic Privilege is speedily dethroned forever!

III. *The God of Religious Formalism.*

The third god who will have to go in the new dis-
pensation after the war, is the God of Religious Formalism. Here we touch something different from
anything which has hitherto been mentioned. The
most shocking thing about the recent collapse of civilisation is the manner in which the principal actors in it
have appealed to religion in order to justify their
unholy actions. They have gone to the Bible, and to
the church and to religion generally in order to justify
every abominable transaction that has taken place in
this chamber of horrors. The customary order of
procedure has been to cut the throats of the Armenians or some other defenceless people and then thank
God for helping in the process; to drop a few bombs
on a church or a group of tenement houses and thank
God again for the results which followed; to let loose
perdition on the battlefield and then go to church and
sing psalms; to pray and then kill; to read the Bible
and then go out and invent a new gas bomb; to sit
down on the field of battle with the stark, blackened,
upturned faces of thousands of men baking in the sun

and write a telegram saying that "with the help of God" we have made an unexampled number of widows and orphans.

In my boyhood days, I used to read Shakespeare's "King Richard the Third," and reflect upon the manner in which that historic ogre would use the name of the Deity in order to forward his plans of murder and assassination. And yet I always realised that Richard was, as Shakespeare intended he should be, an arrant hypocrite. When, for example, he says: "I would to God my heart were flint like Edward's, or Edward's soft and pitiful like mine; I am too childish foolish for this world," while he is plotting murder and assassination, I used to laugh at him, because I knew he was an unconscionable hypocrite, but when William II thanked God, under similar circumstances, I did not laugh for there was little reason to doubt his sincerity. What was wrong with him was his conception of religion. That conception was a part of the old Pagan idea that God is a God of hatred, a God of war, a God of eternal malignancy and destruction. It is characteristic of this idea that it makes the Bible the justification of every sort of Pagan and pre-Christian enormity, and that it makes the chief use of the church and the clergy to secure some sort of spiritual justification for the misdeeds and crimes of the king or of the nation. William of Prussia was educated in schools where this false gospel was taught and, in a sense, he was not to be blamed for imbibing the teaching. The same kind of religious exegesis which made Robert G. Ingersoll an infidel made William II something worse than an infidel—that is, a religious formalist. It is easy for a man to so read and interpret the Bible as to become worse than a heathen. The Pharisees and Sadducees of the time of Christ were great Bible readers, in their own way. They were terribly orthodox on the letter but just as terribly heterodox on the spirit. And the so-called Christian teachers of our own day who are "long" on the slaughter of the Canaanites and the hewing in pieces of Agag, and "short" on the Sermon on the Mount are the Pharisees and Sadducees of the modern age. The religious seminary of the future which purports to be Christian will have to make good its pretensions by showing that its students go out filled with the spirit of Christ, instead of being walking and talking embodiments of a whole host of formalistic and pre-Christian conceptions, the acceptance of which caused the crucifixion of Christ in the first place.

The God of Religious Formalism is dead, and the shrines where he was worshipped, before and during the war, will soon be deserted and will become the habitation of every abominable and unclean thing. It is time to shut them up now and overthrow the idol whose worship has wrought so much havoc for humanity.

IV. *The God of Narrow Nationalism.*

The fourth god who will have to be buried in the near future is the God of Narrow Nationalism. This is the old tribal god of the centuries. He has taught the people of every nation that the people of other nations are inferior and of a lower order of creation as compared with the people of his own nation. He originated such terms as "Gentile" and "Barbarian" and all the other egotistical titles in the nationalistic category. He writes songs like "Deutschland über Alles" and he tries to make his followers believe that because they are themselves therefore they ought to be "über" everybody else. The Apostle Paul had this god in mind when he said, "I am debtor both to the Greeks and to the Barbarians," and again, "In Christ Jesus, there is neither Jew nor Greek, neither bond nor free." Christianity, from the beginning was opposed to the whole spirit of narrow nationalism. It always considered humanity as a whole, never one particular tribe or class or nation. This world would have been spared much misery if it had accepted such an ideal. Instead of doing this, however, it gradually developed a situation of international anarchy which has now reached a point where its further continuance will mean little short of annihilation for the human species.

The whole philosophy of Narrow Nationalism is based upon an absurdity. The people of all nations agree that it is wrong to defraud or rob or murder each other, and that, if these things are done, the wrongdoer must be punished; but the nations which are made up of these same people act on the principle that it is right for a group to do as a group what it is wrong for any individual of the group to do. This is absurd. Thinking people in all nations are now coming to see that there must be international law in

[184]

the future to restrain the criminal actions of the group, just as long ago national law was established within the group to restrain the criminality of the individual. Mr. Wilson in his first war message to Congress put the whole case admirably in these words:

"We are at the beginning of an age in which it will be insisted that the same standards of conduct and responsibility for wrong done shall be observed among nations and their governments that are observed among the individual citizens of civilised states."

Mr. Asquith, the former premier of Great Britain, holds that Narrow Nationalism has completely broken down and that the only hope of the world lies in national disarmament and in some sort of a world court. In an address delivered at Leeds, England, some months ago, he said:

"The limitation of armaments, the acceptance of arbitration as the normal and natural solvent of international disputes, the relegation of wars of ambition and aggression between the States to the same category of obsolete follies in which we class the faction fights of the old republics, the petty conflicts of feudal lords and private duelling—these will be milestones which mark the stages of the road. We must banish once for all from our catalogue of maxims the time-worn fallacy that if you wish for peace you must make ready for war."

Nor is Mr. Asquith alone in these sentiments among the political leaders of his people. Mr. Lloyd George, the present premier of England, said in his address before the British Trades Union, as early as 1918:

"The crushing weight of modern armaments, the increasing evil of compulsory military service, the vast waste of wealth and effort involved in warlike preparation—these are blots on our civilisation, of which every thinking individual must be ashamed. For these and other similar reasons we are confident that a great attempt must be made to establish some international organisation, an alternative to war as a means of settling international disputes."

May we sum up the question with a few words from a recent article by Mr. H. G. Wells, in an American magazine. Mr. Wells says:

"Existing states have become impossible as absolutely independent sovereignties. The new conditions bring them so close together and give them such extravagant powers of mutual injury that they must either sink national pride and dynastic ambitions in subordination to the common welfare of mankind or else utterly shatter one another. It becomes more and more plainly a choice between the League of free nations, and famished men looting in search of non-existent food amidst the burning ruins of our world. In the end I believe that the common sense of mankind will prefer a revision of its ideas of nationality and imperialism, to the latter alternative.

V. *The New World Order.*

The new day of which the poet-prophet of England dreamed nearly a century ago is now dawning. How wonderful these lines seem read in the light of present world conditions:

"For I dipt into the future, far as human eye could see.
  Saw the vision of the world, and all the wonder that
    would be.
  Saw the heaven filled with commerce, argosies of magic
    sails,
  Pilots of the purple twilight, dropping down with costly
    bales;
  Heard the heavens filled with shouting, and there rained a
    ghastly dew
  From the nations' airy navies grappling in the central blue;
  Far along the world wide whisper of the south wind rush-
    ing warm,
  With the standards of the peoples plunging thro' the
    thunder storm;
  Till the war drum throbb'd no longer, and the battle flags
    were furl'd
  In the Parliament of Man, the Federation of the world.
  There the common sense of most shall hold a fretful realm
    in awe,
  And the kindly earth shall slumber, lapt in universal law."

And how still more wonderful seem these lines of the old Hebrew prophet written over two thousand years before Tennyson:

"And he will judge between the nations, and will decide concerning many peoples; and they shall beat their swords into plowshares and their spears into pruning hooks; nation shall not lift up sword against nation, neither shall they learn war any more."

It is, of course, natural that there should still remain a few sceptics in regard to the new world order. One of my friends, who is a member of an organisation which is doing its best to militarise and thereby to Prussianise its native land, belongs to this number. He said to me some while ago that any kind of association of nations is all nonsense, that there have always been wars and they will continue to exist, that those who argue otherwise are dreamers and are not to be taken too seriously. After hearing a good deal of this kind of talk, I disposed of him by reading to him the following resolution of the Lancaster, Ohio, school board passed in 1828, in answer to a request for the use of the schoolhouse for a debate on the practicability of railroads:

"You are welcome to use the schoolroom to debate all proper questions in, but such things as railroads and telegraphs are impossibilities and rank infidelity. There is nothing in the Word of God about them. If God had designed that his intelligent creatures should travel at the frightful speed of fifteen miles an hour by steam, he would have foretold it through His holy prophets. It is a device of Satan to lead immortal souls down to hell."

"Now," I said to him, "you are worse than the Lancaster, Ohio, school board, for they only objected to the era of railroads and telegraphs because they thought such an era had not been prophesied in the Bible. But this new era of internationalism *has* been prophesied in the Bible and standing on the very threshold of it, you still refuse to believe in its appearance."

This is the new age upon which we are entering and no culture is worthy of such an age save a culture which incarnates the spirit of the prophets and dreamers who in the darkness of the past foresaw the glories of the coming dawn. It is fitting, too, that the celebration of the day which history will record as initiating this new order should interpret and emphasise the destruction of the old tribal gods of the past, to the end that mankind might be free to worship and to serve the True and Living God of the future!

XVI

GRATITUDE, TRUE AND FALSE

(*A Thanksgiving Sermon*)

TEXT: *Luke* 18:11. "God, I thank thee."

THE custom of Thanksgiving is very old. The idea of setting apart a special day for returning thanks to the Deity goes back to the most primitive times. The Egyptians, Jews, Greeks and Romans all held festivals and various religious exercises devoted to the idea of Thanksgiving. The Hellenic goddess of the harvest, Demeter, was supposed to preside over the Greek Thanksgiving day; while the Latin goddess of nature, Ceres, occupied a similar position in the religious life of the Romans. Throughout European history, we read of days specially set apart as times of rejoicing over victories and as occasions of special Thanksgiving. It was in fact the usual thing for the church to consecrate a certain number of days during the year to fasting, thanksgiving and prayer. During the reign of Elizabeth in England, many such occasions are noted. An especially well-known thanksgiving day and probably one which had decided influence in helping to establish our own celebration was the one observed in Leyden, Holland, on October third. This date commemorated the raising of the siege of the city by the Spaniards in 1575. The fact that many of the Pilgrim fathers had lived in Holland and that they established the Thanksgiving custom less than fifty years after the siege of Leyden would seem to indicate that the well-known Holland festival furnished the immediate prototype for its American successor.

There are three thanksgiving days in American history which stand out with especial pre-eminence. First, the thanksgiving of the Pilgrims at Plymouth in November, 1621, when the colonists gave thanks for the harvest they had garnered after a year of the most extreme suffering and hardships. Second, the first national thanksgiving day observed on November 26, 1789, by proclamation of Washington. Third, the thanksgiving day of November, 1863, established by Abraham Lincoln, and since his time observed as an annual festival. Previous to the Lincoln proclamation, Thanksgiving day had been observed upon exceptional occasions only; but since 1863 it has been the uniform practice of our chief executives to call the people together for thanksgiving and prayer on the last Thursday in November of every year. There are certain passages in the proclamation of Lincoln which are worth remembering. Among other things he says:

"The year that is drawing toward its close has been filled with the blessings of fruitful fields and healthful skies. To these bounties, which are so constantly enjoyed that we are prone to forget the source from which they come, others have been added which are of so extraordinary nature that they cannot fail to penetrate and soften even the heart which is habitually insensible to the ever-watchful providence of Almighty God. No human counsel hath devised nor hath any mortal hand worked out these great things. They are the gracious gifts of the Most High God, who, while dealing with us in anger for our sins, hath nevertheless remembered mercy."

I. *True Versus False Thanksgiving*.

The text which has been selected for our consideration will doubtless appear out of place to many. It is a portion of the well-known prayer of the Pharisee contained in Christ's parable of the Pharisee and the publican as narrated in the Gospel of Luke. It has been selected as the basis of this sermon because it stands out as pre-eminently typical of a form of thanksgiving which is unfortunately far from rare in human history. Like all other religious customs, thanksgiving tends to become a formality and very often we assume, albeit unconsciously, the Pharisaical attitude. It is difficult to preserve the spirit of genuine gratitude so long as our attention is centred upon the acquirement of material advantages or the building up of a fortune or even a competency for ourselves. The great fault about the prayer of the Pharisee was that it had no touch of unselfishness in it. The man was proud of his gains, proud of his character, proud of his standing in the community, proud of his intellectual ability, in short, his attitude reflected the acme of selfish satisfaction.

As a nation and as individuals, we need constantly

to examine ourselves to see whether our thanksgiving
is true and genuine, or whether we have gravitated, at
least, toward the hypocritical gratitude of the Pharisee.
It is to such an examination that we are called to-day.
In order to enter into it in the proper sort of way, it
is necessary that we should understand fully the issues
which are involved.

II. *False Thanksgiving—The Test.*

The test of Pharisaical thanksgiving is the possession of a fundamentally selfish attitude. Whenever we
feel that we are better than others and that our own
goodness makes us immune so far as responsibility for
helping others is concerned, we are putting ourselves
in a position to pray like the Pharisee. There was
perhaps never a time in the history of our nation when
we were more tempted to take this attitude than we are
to-day. Beyond any question, we are far and away the
richest nation on earth. From the standpoint of military prowess, we have replaced Germany in the
thought of the world. Our people have better educational facilities, greater material comforts and greater
opportunities for advancement than are enjoyed by any
other people on the globe. We complain about taxes
and the burdens of war, but the fact is that in comparison with other civilised nations we are fortunate beyond calculation. Our debt per capita is only a small
fraction of the staggering burden which the war has
imposed upon other and less fortunate nations.

Under circumstances such as these, there is great

temptation for us to rejoice in our own good fortune and to thank God that we are not like the others. The fruitage of such an attitude is found in our unwillingness to risk any comfort or convenience in order to help our neighbours. During the earlier years of the war, the idealism of our people was challenged with the statement, almost universally heralded throughout the land, that we were engaged in an unselfish struggle to destroy militarism, to make the world safe for democracy, and to drive the spirit of war from the globe forever. If there were those who did not believe in these idealistic pronouncements, they said nothing about their doubts. Any one who was familiar with the general attitude of the people cannot dispute the fact that during the earlier days of the war the public, as a whole, was appealed to almost entirely from the standpoint of unselfish and idealistic considerations. Moreover, the response to such appeals was enthusiastic and overwhelming.

Now, however, we are told that we went into the war to save our own skins and that our motives were cold-bloodedly selfish. By the same token, we are instructed to look out for our own interests in all matters pertaining to world reconstruction, regardless of what may happen to the rest of humanity. We are to thank God that the Atlantic separated us, in large measure, from the world conflagration, and we are to take care to use to the fullest the advantage which our good fortune has given us in the game of world politics. If we listen to our counsellors who argue after this fashion, it will mean that we will be pilloried before the world as the Pharisee of the nations. Even before the war, our love of money and the atmosphere of materialism which surrounded our national life gave our pretensions of religion and virtue a Pharisaical cast in the eyes of many other peoples. We cannot afford to confirm such impressions by assuming the selfish attitude at this crisis in world history.

III. *The Danger of False Thanksgiving.*

Both from the national and from the individual viewpoint, we face no greater danger than is involved in the keynote of this sermon. We have many virtues, as a people, and we have many things of which we may well be proud. So had the Pharisee. There is no question but that he was, externally at least, a rather exceptionally decent character. The Biblical account of his prayer in no way impeaches the accuracy of his statements concerning his own virtues. At a time when most people were grossly derelict with regard to the moral law, he could say, no doubt truthfully, that he was not like the common crowd. He did not steal, he did not cheat, he was clean in his personal life, he did not even engage in shady transactions like the publican beneath his feet. Moreover, his virtues were by no means negative. He fasted twice a week and he contributed regularly of his earthly goods to the church. What more can America say of herself? We are accustomed to a good deal of self-praise in the matter of our national history. Probably we are better off than most other nations, but we do not have too much of which to boast. For one thing, we are still in our infancy as compared with most of the others. By the testimony of our own historians, there are certain features, connected with at least one of our wars, which will not stand too much scrutiny. Our recent diplomatic dealings with the United States of Colombia will not help us in the eyes of people of other nations. Before oil was discovered in large quantities in Colombia, we indignantly repudiated the claims for indemnity made upon us. We stood upon our honour and asserted that to pay the amount asked for would mean a confession of national guilt in connection with the digging of the Panama Canal. Some of our lawmakers were almost furious in their attacks upon their comrades who would even suggest compromising our national integrity by the payment of a single dollar under the circumstances mentioned. So matters stood until the news came that an oil field, rivalling the Tampico section, was in process of development in Colombia. Almost over night, our belligerent lawmakers had a change of heart. The national honour, in their judgment, ran no risk of being compromised by paying the indemnity to Colombia. Notwithstanding the pressure of after-war obligations and the desire to placate the people, hungry for tax relief, the twenty-five million indemnity passed our Congress by an overwhelming majority.

The Colombia incident is but one out of numerous examples of the influence of monetary consideration in shaping our national policies. It is this sort of thing which has made America synonymous with the worship of money in the eyes of citizens of other nations. The contributions made through the Hoover Relief Committees, and in other ways, have helped to change this impression; but after all we have given so little in comparison with what we could give and ought to give that the more unpleasant criticism still remains.

IV. *The Nature of True Thanksgiving.*

We need the attitude of the publican, rather than the attitude of the Pharisee, as we approach our day of national thanksgiving. In the face of our responsibilities to the world, we should be humble instead of assuming the attitude of self-righteousness. There are so many outstretched hands from the needy ones of the world that, until they are filled, we should have little cause for self-gratulation. It is useless for us to pride ourselves upon our superior virtue or our superior wealth so long as we do not use these gifts to better the condition of others. After all, whatever superiority may be ours at this time is largely the result of chance and not of any merit of our own. If we really possess the spirit of thanksgiving, we ought to show that spirit by whole-hearted sacrifice in the interest of our neighbours.

If we hearken to our jingo press and to a certain type of political leadership which always appeals to selfish and immediate interests, our thanksgiving prayer to-day will be something like this: "God, I thank thee that we are not extortioners, like the Germans, nor unjust, like the English, nor unclean, like the Japanese, nor even like this publican which we call Soviet

Russia. We Americans go to church more than the rest; we do not exactly give tithes, but we contribute, at least a portion of our wealth, to religion; and we have even given a small fraction of what we spend every year in trivial amusements to the starving people across the seas who are constantly begging us for relief."

I wonder whether we are ready to assume this attitude or whether we are not ready to say something like this: "Lord, we are richer than any other people; we have natural advantages which make us exceptionally favoured among the nations; we are a great commonwealth and we have in our hands the power to do almost anything for world betterment that we may desire. In spite of all these gifts, gifts which we acknowledge come from Thee, we have done almost nothing to relieve the suffering and want of other and less favoured peoples. We claim to be a Christian nation, but we have made no attempt to practise the teachings of Christ in our dealings with others. As we think of our obligations and the pitiably inadequate manner in which we have fulfilled them, there is only one prayer which fits our condition and that is the prayer of the publican, God, be merciful to us for we are sinners."

Surely upon an occasion such as this, we can do no better than recall those words of Kipling in "The Recessional":

"If drunk with sight of power, we loose
　Wild tongues that have not Thee in awe,
Such boasting as the Gentiles use
　Or lesser breeds without the law—

[198]

Lord God of Hosts, be with us yet,
Lest we forget—lest we forget!"

"For heathen heart that puts her trust
    In reeking tube and iron shard,
All valiant dust that builds on dust,
    And guarding calls not Thee to guard,
For frantic boast and foolish word,
Thy mercy on Thy people, Lord!"

XVII

THE PROBLEM OF SUFFERING; AS RELATED TO THE INCARNATION

(*A Christmas Sermon*)

TEXT: *John* 3:16. "For God so loved the world."

IN that masterpiece of language and thought springing out of the birth-throes of what was really a great soul, the book entitled "De Profundis" written by Oscar Wilde while a prisoner in Reading Gaol, there is a sentence something like this, "There is enough suffering in one narrow London lane to show that God does not love man, and wherever there is any sorrow, though but that of a child in some little garden weeping over a fault that it has or has not committed, the whole face of creation is completely marred."

I. *The Problem Stated.*

It is true that Wilde reverses his verdict a little later in the book, but the striking power of the illustration remains the same. The hardest thing in the world for me to believe is the fact of the goodness of God. The most difficult text in the Bible to explain is the statement that "God so loved the world." I do not find it difficult personally to believe in a miracle. Life itself is the supreme miracle, and I am sure of life, but to stand in the presence of the awful wretchedness, misery, and wrong of the world and then to say that the Being who made all this loved it and loved man; this is hard to understand. I wonder if that Cincinnati mother understood it of whom the papers told a few years ago. Out of work; a widow, with three small mouths to feed and nothing to feed them, after struggling with her agony for days, she at last takes the lives of her children to spare them further pain, and then her own. As her starving, agonised gaze looked up through her garret window into the bleak, unpitying heavens, there must have been something in her approaching the Divine if she could believe in a loving God. Surely one life like hers will weigh down much of the smug and self-complacent optimism of the classes which let her starve.

No one can pursue in the slightest measure the study of anthropology, the science of man, or of archæology, the science of everything that is old, without being impressed with the heartlessly brutal character of the early peoples from whom we have sprung. There is a sort of grim, fantastic horror about those old Assyrian tablets immortalised in the prosaic and dingy courts of the British Museum. One sees people being burned alive and impaled and flayed and having their eyes put out on every side. And the Assyrians were the cultured people of the older days. Of the barbarity of the early stages of the world's history, it is almost impossible to conceive. When one reflects that crucifixion was the legalised punishment of the most civilised nation of the world for nearly a thousand years, he can form some faint idea of what took place in barbarous lands.

To the student of biology, no less than the anthropologist or the archæologist, the problem seems to present insuperable difficulties. It is not that we find exceptional cases of cruelty, murder, and lust as we go back farther and farther in our study of the various forms of life, but rather that life itself seems based upon an utter indifference to these things. The struggle for existence means simply that the strong have always conquered the weak; that the unpitying arm of might has always prevailed. Out of an innumerable offspring, Nature selects the few strongest types and bids the rest perish from her sight. It is little wonder that Professor Haeckel should style the process an immoral one, and should laugh at the idea of there being either duty or love back of the universe.

Much that is in our present day civilisation presents a similar antinomy. It is only the shallow thinker, the man or the woman whose butterfly existence has never probed the heart of things who can look at the world even as it is to-day without a certain soberness of mien and even sadness of heart. I was much impressed a few years ago when I read that report of the Charity Organization Society of New York dealing with conditions of living among the labouring classes in the city of Pittsburgh. One reads of the almost certain doom of labourers following various crafts for a livelihood; of work so exceedingly deadly that no form of protective insurance has yet been able to be devised, however high the rate imposed; of tenement houses owned by a corporation with a capital stock of over a billion dollars, and yet of which, to quote the exact language of the report, "for us to have found a more humanly destructive group of bad houses would have been impossible." These labourers, doomed to slow death by consumption, often surrounded by families which they must leave uncared for, looking up with their last gaze into the wan faces of wife or child, left alone in the busy, pitiless world; these men, I say, may well cry out in agony of soul, "How can it be that the God who made us and made the world could have loved us?"

One of the peculiarly striking experiences of my life, one which is still etched, as it were, with a sort of indelible acid upon my soul, is a scene which I witnessed during the first month of my ministry. I was summoned to the bedside of a woman dying of quick consumption. She was young, not yet twenty. Her husband and one child, a little girl, would survive her. As I tried in the most quiet, sympathetic way I could command to comfort her in her wretchedness with the thought of God's love, she turned to me and whispered, for she could no longer speak aloud, "Does God love me? Then why doesn't he help me?" Somehow those words took the answer out of my lips. I could not help thinking of how utterly impossible it was for me, strong, vigorous, active, happy, to talk of God's love to her. I tried to put myself in her place, and wondered whether I would not see it in the same way, and often since that time, as I have passed along through the world, drinking its nectar and tasting its manifold delights, suddenly a pale, wan face comes before me and a quick, feverish whisper says again, "Does God love me? Then why doesn't he help me?"

In the face of these problems, the statement of Christianity that God is love appears so strange and paradoxical that it demands an explanation. If God loves the world, surely his has been a strange way of showing his love. Strange love, which tortures its own children, which condemns them pitilessly to rack and faggot and cross, which dooms them to days of wretchedness and nights of tears, to misery of body and despair of soul, to poverty and grief and misery and distress and want. Strange love, indeed. And if this be God's, the very best that can be said of it is that it is not like our own.

II. *The Problem Solved Through the Incarnation.*

Is there, then, any way of understanding how God can love the world in the face of all these things? There is a great saying in the Gospel of John, perhaps the most familiar saying in the Bible, "For God so loved the world that he gave his only begotten Son." I do not believe that the full significance of those words is often appreciated. They furnish to me the one and only solution of the problem of world suffering and sorrow. There was a time in my religious development when the idea of the deity of Christ seemed like an inexplicable thing. It seemed almost irreverent to me, as it always seemed to the Greeks, that God himself should die upon the cross. That God should suffer bitter torture at the hands of his own creatures seemed like an unthinkable, almost a hideous thing. As I have thought deeper, however, into the heart of the world problem, I have come to realise that the only possible solution of the eternal mystery lies precisely in the cross. If God who made the world with its misery is willing himself to share that misery, nay sound it to its very depths, then after all he may have loved the thing he made. A general may seem harsh and cruel to his soldiers when he orders them on forced marches and exposes them to bitter privation, but when he himself goes down into the ranks and suffers with them and shares the bitterest lot they have to share, then they come to realise that the harsh orders were given for a purpose and that after all their general cares for them and loves them. And so in the suffering Saviour I discern a suffering God. In the last bitter agony of Gethsemane and Calvary I see God voluntarily enduring all the misery his creatures have to endure, draining their bitterest cup to the dregs just in order to show them that however they may misunderstand his universe, he yet loves them with an infinite love.

The atonement thus becomes not the old and to me impossible idea of Christ atoning to God for the sins of the world, but it becomes rather the new and magnificently sublime idea of God atoning to the world for whatever suffering their creation may have brought upon His people. It is for this reason that the divinity of Christ becomes so necessary in the Christian economy. Take it away, and the whole world problem is an insoluble mystery; grant it, and light illumines the gloom. I frankly confess that there is no escape from pessimism for me except through the cross. The God who made the world is either a heartless God or he is Christ. No man who thinks things through can reach any other conclusion. "God so loved the world that he gave his only begotten son" are the key words which unlock the riddle of the universe.

III. *A Further Problem—Why Suffering at All?*

But having reached at least some solution of the great mystery through the cross, there arises another problem which demands an answer. Why, it may be asked, is there any need at all for suffering? Why could there not have been a world in which neither the Creator nor his creatures would need to suffer? Could not the Almighty by a single touch of His omnipotent hand or a single word from his life-giving lips have breathed into existence a universe where sorrow should be unknown and where sadness should die still-born and never see the light? Could not the Omnipotent have made roses without thorns, pleasure without pain, and innocence without a suspicion of guilt? One answer to these questions, it seems to me, must forever silence criticism. The cross proves the existence of Omnipotent Love, and Omnipotent Love has not made a thornless universe. Therefore it could not be made without sacrificing something greater in order to secure it. Everything in life points to something higher than mere feeling values. Pleasure is good and pain bad, but pleasure is neither the highest good nor is pain the greatest evil. The supreme values are character values and these are often independent of either pleasure or pain. Somehow we feel that the good life must be ultimately the happy life, but it is only ultimately that it becomes so, and before the goal is reached much of pain must enter into the process.

This truth, so hard for us to believe, or to understand, has always received the approval of the great and the good of the world. The supreme genius of William Shakespeare recognised it as the result of the painful travail of many years. Shakespeare in his youth delighted in characters of sunny temper and cloudless smiles, in maidens like the fair-browed Rosalind or the witty Beatrice dwelling in a fairy land of ambrosial raptures and with hearts untouched by a single scar. But out of the crucible of the sonnet years came forth the riper testimony of the seer. Bitter indeed are the crucifixions of Hamlet and Othello and Lear, terrible are the martyrdoms of the saints who stepped forth aureole-crowned from their pages to take their places in the Pantheon of fame. And yet these characters: Cordelia, Desdemona, Hamlet, we recognise at once as the supreme monument of the poet's genius and power. Surely had Shakespeare created a world, he would not have made it a thornless one. With him, too, the supreme values are character values, and these are always wrought out of the furnace of pain.

In the book from which I quoted at the beginning of this sermon, the "De Profundis" of Oscar Wilde,

there is a similar testimony. Wilde acknowledges that
he, like Shakespeare, and I suppose like every one
else, for many years could not understand the strange
combination of love and suffering in the world. But
later through much tribulation and tears, he reaches
a truer view of things. "Now," he says, "it seems
to me that love of some kind is the only possible explanation of the extraordinary amount of suffering
there is in the world. "I am convinced," he continues,
"that there is no other explanation and that if the
world has indeed, as I have said, been built of sorrow,
it has been built by the hands of love because in no
other way could the soul of man for whom the world
was made reach the full stature of its perfection.
Pleasure for the beautiful body, but pain for the beautiful soul."

IV. *The True Optimism.*

So it is that we come with chastened speech and
trembling lips by the way that leads to Golgotha over
into the eternal kingdom of the blessed life. Through
tears of shame and agonies of humiliation we grope
our way upward to the stars. We kiss the rod, knowing that its keenest sting comes from the very heart
of God. Through boundless faith and endless hope
we press onward to the courts of love. Yes, had God
made everything easy for us, how little indeed had he
loved us!

And yet while we realise the truthfulness of these
things, it is still hard to cling to them. As another

has said, 'Far off, like a perfect pearl one can see the city of God. It is so wonderful that it seems as if a child could reach it in a summer day. But with us it is so hard to hold heights that the soul is competent to gain. Yet must we keep our faces set toward the gate which is called beautiful though we fall many times and often in the mist go astray.' It is much, I take it, after all, to have had the vision even though at times it fades away. It is much to be able when we think our best to see love at the heart of the world. It is much to see the glory of God in those twilight reveries of thought which help us to peer for a moment across the bar and into the infinite beyond. As Whittier has said,

> "The clouds that rise, with thunders slake
> Our thirsty souls with rain;
> The blow most dreaded falls to break
> From off our limbs a chain,
> And wrongs of man to man but make
> The love of God more plain,
> As through the shadowy lens of even
> The eye looks farthest into heaven,
> One dreams of stars and depths of blue
> The glaring sunshine never knew."

If moral, that is to say ideal, values are alone worth while in the world, and if in order to secure them pain and suffering must needs be endured, then after all there is a firm and solid basis for the only optimism that is worth while,—the optimism which does not dodge difficulties, but which faces them through to the end. This is the optimism of Cordelia, of Desdemona, of Hamlet, of Rabbi ben Ezra, and of Saul. Browning, like Fichte, and like Paul, even rejoices in tribulations, seeing in them the only possible means of reaching the higher goal. In that vigorous, almost super-robust style which has made him famous, he:

"Welcomes each rebuff that turns earth's smoothness rough;
 That bids nor stand nor sit, but go;
 Be our joys three parts pain,
 Strive and hold cheap the strain,
 Learn, nor account the pang; dare, never grudge the throe."

Perhaps some of us with less physical vigour than Browning and a more contemplative and sober turn of mind may find an easier truth in the simpler, though no less charming words of Whitcomb Riley:

"O, the rain and the sun, and the sun and the rain!
 When the tempest is done, then the sun-shine again,
 And in rapture we'll ride through the stormiest gales,
 For God's hand's on the helm and his breath's in the sails.
 Then murmur no more in lull or in roar,
 But smile and be brave, till the voyage is o'er."

Yes, of a truth, whether it seems quite true to us at all times or not, the Lord *is* our Shepherd. He leads us through the parched desert sometimes no less than by the still waters, but always he leads us on. Before us is the cup which runneth over; the table loaded with bounties; the stillness and peace of the Father's presence forever. The same John who wrote "For God so loved the world" wrote also on the Isle of Patmos, as he gazed upon the glorious host of the redeemed, "These are they who have come up out of great tribulation and have washed their robes and made them white in the blood of the Lamb."

"Once in every man's life," says Oscar Wilde, "he

walks with Christ to Emmaus." Shall we not walk with Him as we leave this house on the day sacred to His Incarnation and to his glorious advent in the world!

XVIII

THE END OF THE HARVEST

(*Sermon for the Last Day of the Year*)

TEXT: *Jer.* 8:20. "The harvest is past, the summer is ended, and we are not saved."

IN a few more hours, the current year will have passed into history. There is something solemn about the moment of death, be it only the death of the year. As the minutes slowly tick away, something is passing which will never return again. The old year is dying. Spring with her garlands of roses will deck his brow no more; Summer with her rich fruitage and harvest has gone forever; Autumn's golden haze is a thing of the past. Peace be to the dying year. We consign him to the earth, and with a tear for those who have died with him and who were near and dear to us, we pronounce the words, "earth to earth, dust to dust, ashes to ashes," and with bowed heads we pass from his grave.

Some of us will recall with what hopes and ambitions the year which is now dying began. How we dreamed of this or the other thing which should be achieved before it closed; how we said to ourselves, "when the dawn of another year comes, I shall be thus much richer, or better, or happier than I am to-day." And to-night we strike the balance and find out how far we have succeeded in our expectations. For most of us at least, some things have not been realised. Unexpected disappointments have come, those accidents of fortune which seem impossible to foresee or to avoid—death, disease, something which smote the sinews of our arms and made it impossible for us to reach the goal. Or it may be, that our own carelessness or indolence, or lack of energy, or all of them put together, were responsible for the failure.

As we look back upon the past, perhaps we can see mistakes which might have been avoided, bits of blundering and folly, that tripped our feet and hurled us headlong, things which we ought to have seen but failed to see, thorns which prick all the more bitterly to-night because there might have been roses in their place. How we wish we could unsay the harsh word which caused so much trouble for us or for others, or undo the rash action, the consequences of which were so much more serious than we anticipated. Whatever the cause, now that our time is up, we recognise the failure. With that instinct of hopefulness which is the mainstay of life, we say that what we failed to do during the last year, we shall do during the year to come. But this is an impossibility. We may do something like what we purposed for the past year, but we shall not achieve the past purpose itself. The opportunity to do that closed with the year. However successful the future may be, the failures of the past cannot be wiped out; they remain failures and shall so remain until the crash of doom. The books have been

[213]

closed; the account has been balanced; the time for payment has expired; we are declared defaulters for the year.

I. *The Lesson of the Year, the Lesson of Life.*

What is true of the past year, will be true of each of our lives, in greater or less proportion. As the account for this year in a few hours will be made up; so, some day, just when neither you nor the angels in heaven know, the account for your life will be made up; the books will be closed, and however much you may desire to undo the past or unmake a record already made, your efforts will be fruitless and vain.

The words of the text refer to just such a regretful survey on the part of a nation which had neglected opportunities until they had passed forever. From his place as a prophet in the dying agonies of the idolatrous kingdom of Judah, looking forward to the years of captivity near at hand, above all, to that destruction of national freedom which should never terminate, in tones of bitter regret, Jeremiah pronounces the fateful words, "the harvest is past, the summer is ended, and we are not saved." In one short sentence, he summarises the doom of his people. No other words could convey quite so well the hopelessness of their fate. "The harvest is past." "The opportunities for work and service have flown." "The summer is ended." The time in which we may work is no more. Life presents just these two conditions out of which we must all mould our fates: these two and no

[214]

more. Let us note briefly just what each of them means to you and to me, no less than what they meant to Jeremiah or to Judah.

II. *The Meaning of the Harvest.*

First then, let us observe that the harvest is a period for the display of strength and energy. Some years ago, Doctor William Osler, Regius Professor of Medicine in Oxford University, caused a great sensation by his statement that after forty years of age a man's opportunities, so far as originating anything, great or useful in the world are practically at an end. There was much harsh criticism of a pronouncement which was very largely misunderstood. Doctor Osler did not mean that old people were useless, or of no value, or that they ought to be put out of the road; as some editors and magazine writers tried to make us believe. What he meant was, that there are ten or twenty years in a man's life when his faculties are all at their best; when his nerves are strongest and his brain clearest; when his memory is unclouded and his will firm. If he dilly-dallies with opportunities during these years; if he puts off doing anything worthwhile until his old age; when old age comes, it will not meet his expectations. There is a time for harvest, a time to thrust in the sickle and to bind up the sheaves. Let the harvest time pass by, and the crop, whatever it may be, is ruined forever. By and by, the muscles will become weaker; the nerves less firm; the limbs unsteady, and harvest time will be almost over. What kind of sheaves are we bearing with us as we totter out of this world into the next? Are they sheaves of golden grain, which will stand the test of the flail, or are they tares worthy only of being burned?

III. *Harvest, a Period of Opportunity*.

Again, I observe, that the harvest season is a period of opportunity. We are given strength and ability to garner the grain and we are also given grain to garner. It would be useless to try to number or to name the various opportunities which are ours. This world is a tremendous harvest field with all kinds of grain ready to be garnered. There are sections labelled "Wealth," "Pleasure," "Ambition," "Power," and the like. The most important of all is the harvest of the future. "Shall I live for the Now, or for the Hereafter?" is the most significant question before any human being. By and by the time will come when choosing will be no longer possible. Then I shall have leisure for regret but for nothing more. To-day is the harvest period.

Not long ago, a young girl in one of our eastern cities shot and killed the man who was about to desert her and then committed suicide. In the letter which she left behind her, she stated that she had at one time been a member of one of the oldest churches in the city in which she lived. One line of the letter was singularly pathetic: "Do not tell my mother," she wrote, "what an awful failure her daughter has made of life." A few years before, the world with all its countless opportunities was hers: it was her time for harvest.

Out of the numberless paths before her, she chose one that led downward; soon her harvest was ended; and what a harvest it was with which to enter eternity!

Why is it that people regret so bitterly the mistaken lives of the past? The career is ended. For better or worse, the history has been written. There is nothing more now that can be done: why then, lament and weep over the impossible? Is not the reason found in the fact that we all recognise when too late, how perfectly easy it would have been for us to have achieved something different from what was the actual result of our efforts? We see, when too late, how easy it would have been, if we had cared to have it so for us to have become another man or another woman from what we are. Why is it that with our shrivelled sheaves in our hands we shrink from facing the Master of the Harvest? There are those who say that everything happens just as it would have happened anyway, and if a man garners thistles instead of wheat, it is something that could not have been otherwise. But if this were true, no man would ever be afraid to stand before the judgment bar of God, and conscience and remorse and regret would become hideous mysteries impossible to explain. We may salve our souls, and justify our misdeeds with thoughts of the kind, but at the last they will not stand the test of the refiner's fire or the thresher's flail. The common sense of mankind brushes aside all such metaphysical sophistry. Man created in the image of God, can and does make or mar his own destiny. If we are lost, it is our own fault and we know it. Look back over the events of the past year;

there is the blunder, we will say, that you made when you chose a certain bargain instead of another. Did you have to choose the one you did? Somebody may try to argue you into that idea, but you know better, and it is because you know better that you hate to think of the blunder.

What is true of a simple blunder, is very much more true of a crime. We feel regret for our blunders; we feel remorse for our sins. Moreover, what is true of a single action, or a single year, is very much more true of a lifetime. Some one has said that there ought to be no thinking done at the moment of death; the thinking should all be done beforehand. John Randolph, the great American statesman, in his last illness, said to his doctor: "Remorse! remorse! remorse! Let me see the word! show it to me in the dictionary!" There being none in the room, he said to the doctor: "Write it then." The doctor wrote in on both sides of the card, at Randolph's direction. It was then underlined, as he wished it. He gazed upon it, and then said: "Remorse! You don't know what it means! you don't know what it means!" And so people may talk about the folly of saying that things could be otherwise than they are, as much as they please, but in the hour of death their own consciences contradict them. There was a certain philosopher who tried to argue Diogenes into the belief that motion is an illusion, and that reason proves it to be impossible. Diogenes listened to the argument and then got up and walked across the room. "What are you doing that for?" said his friend. "To prove to you that I can move whether motion is impossible or not," he replied. So men may argue themselves into almost any state of mind, but before God and the Angel of Death their arguments fade away. The great facts of experience testify that conscience and remorse and regret are real, and actual, and dependent upon our own behaviour. To-day, the harvest field is open before us to choose whatever we will; to-morrow we can only approve or regret the choice we have made. Let us be careful, therefore, how we choose to-day. Opportunities fade away as strength becomes weaker. When both have gone, the harvest is over. If the harvest of the past year should be our life harvest, would the results be satisfactory to us? if not, why not? No man knows the measure of his days: it may yet be that this harvest shall be the harvest of life for us.

IV. *Harvest and Time.*

The passing of the harvest constitutes one side of the text but there is another. Life not only means the use of strength and opportunities, but it also means time in which to use them. People sometimes say that they do not know what to do in order to while away time; but if they possess any measure of strength or opportunity they are very silly persons to use such language. The wise man or the wise woman has not too much time, but rather too little. The days, the weeks, the months, the years, flit by in a whirlwind of motion, until at last our hands are crossed in death, and time for us is no more. The summer is ended.

Very precious the hours become as they draw near the end. A rich Philadelphian, it is said, paid his physician at the rate of six thousand dollars an hour to keep him alive a few days longer, and he was scarcely more than half alive then. People have offered fabulous sums for a few hours more of life. While health continues and everything goes well, time may hang heavy on our hands, as we sometimes say, but that state of mind is not permanent. As the summer draws near the end, we see so many things to do, and so little time in which to do them. In the bright June days, we idled away the precious hours; we disregarded warnings and admonitions, but now we haven't a moment to attend to those things which we see are absolutely needful. Let no one despise Time, lest a moment come when he shall pray heaven and earth for only a day longer in which to attempt to rebuild his life.

A metropolitan journal told the other day of a man who died in an eastern city, some years ago, leaving a fortune of eleven millions of dollars. On his death bed, he constantly gave expression to his remorse for what his conscience told him had been an illspent life: "If I could only live my life over again," he said, "if I could only be spared for a few years, I would give all the wealth I have amassed in a lifetime." High prices have been paid for various things in the history of the world, but nothing has brought a higher price than time. Is it not the part of wisdom to use it properly when it is given you as God's gift free as the air of heaven? Precious is the gold with its power of purchasing the varied good things of life; precious is the diamond with its star-like rays of never-dying lustre: precious are all of the numberless treasures of the world, but there is none of them so precious as the fleeting moments of time. The ticking of a watch is like the tolling of a bell. The sunset of a single day is but a prophecy of the sunset of life. The snows of winter which fall year after year upon the graves of those we loved in the village church-yard in mute but eloquent language speak to us of the passing of the summer time of our own lives. Soon for us, like them, the summer will have ended. Winter, bleak winter, will be upon us, and the night wherein no man can work. Shall the refrain of our lives be the mournful refrain of Jeremiah: "the harvest is past, the summer is ended, and we are not saved"?

V. *The Conclusion.*

We are not saved. Yes, that is the great and important feature of the whole sentence. Harvest, and summer-time have existed for a purpose. We have not used them to that end. The broad fields so rich with precious grain, have invited us in vain. The course of our lives has been turned awry by our own free volition. We all owe a three-fold duty in this world; a duty to God, a duty to our fellow-man, a duty to ourselves. We have slighted our duty to God; have refused allegiance to him; have rejected the offers of admission to his Kingdom. We have not lived for our fellow-men as we should have lived; there were cases where we could have shown our brotherhood and

did not do it; now it is all over, and the little money
we saved, it may be, as the result of our selfish policy,
is not worth while. In the closing hours of life, the
thought of unselfish goodness is sweet to the soul: in
those moments, we do not remember our sharp strokes
of diplomacy, but rather our strokes that were more
honest and not quite so sharp. It is in that hour that
the man who has been cheated more than evens up with
the man who has cheated him. Failing in our duty
to God, and to our fellow-man, we cannot but have
failed in our duty to our own higher selves. It is a
strange sort of truth, but none the less a very clear one
that the man who thinks only of his own self never has
a self worth thinking of. We have despised God; we
have been uncharitable to man, all for the sake of self,
and now we have a self that is afraid to face the judgment. There is something sadly pathetic about the
negative ring of the words: "we are not saved." How
easy, during the harvest times, to have kept the "not"
out of the sentence: how impossible to take it out now
that the harvest is past.

I have often thought that the saddest of all things in
this world are the things that we miss, the things we
lose; not the terrible battles we have to face, not the
conflicts of body or of soul, but the might-have-beens
that are not; the paradises which, by our own deliberate
folly, we threw away. Like shadows we pass from
this world into the next; our life is but a vapour which
fleeth away. "In the morning we are like grass which
groweth up. In the morning it flourisheth, and groweth up; in the evening it is cut down, and withereth."

The harvest is not for long, if every opportunity is seized; the summer is soon ended, even though we do not waste a day. But for us who neglect the opportunities and let the days pass by unheeded, some time, when too late, there shall come the refrain of Jeremiah: "The harvest is passed, the summer is ended, and we are not saved."

THE END

F. H.